When Family Businesses are Best

When Family Businesses are Best

The Parallel Planning Process for Family Harmony and Business Success

Randel S. Carlock
Berghmans Lhoist Chaired Professor in
Entrepreneurial Leadership
and Founding Director of the Wendel International
Centre for Family Enterprise, INSEAD

and

John L. Ward
Clinical Professor and Co-Director, Center for Family
Enterprises, Kellogg School of Management,
Northwestern University

First published 2010 by
PALGRAVE MACMILLAN

Palgrave Macmillan in the UK is an imprint of Macmillan Publishers Limited, registered in England, company number 785998, of Houndmills, Basingstoke, Hampshire RG21 6XS.

Palgrave Macmillan in the US is a division of St Martin's Press LLC, 175 Fifth Avenue, New York, NY 10010.

Palgrave Macmillan is the global academic imprint of the above companies and has companies and representatives throughout the world.

Palgrave® and Macmillan® are registered trademarks in the United States, the United Kingdom, Europe and other countries.

ISBN 978-0-230-22262-5

This book is printed on paper suitable for recycling and made from fully managed and sustained forest sources. Logging, pulping and manufacturing processes are expected to conform to the environmental regulations of the country of origin.

A catalogue record for this book is available from the British Library.

A catalog record for this book is available from the Library of Congress.

10 9 8 7 6 5 4 3 2
19 18 17 16 15 14 13 12 11 10

Printed and bound in Great Britain by
MPG Group, Bodmin and Kings Lynn

This book is dedicated to all the students, executives, and business families from around the world that have studied and shared ideas with us over the past years. Your energy and enthusiasm support our efforts.

Contents

List of Figures

List of Tables

Acknowledgments

As this book is an interdisciplinary effort, we would like to recognize the support of our teams at INSEAD and Kellogg.

The INSEAD Wendel International Centre for Family Enterprise (of which Professor Carlock is the founding director) is staffed by center coordinators Veronique Sanciaume and Nathalie Bogacz. We are also extremely grateful to the Berghmans, Lhoist, Hoffmann, and Wendel families who early on recognized the importance of our work and provided the financial support that made our research and writing possible. The support of the Berghmans Lhoist Chair in Entrepreneurial Leadership provides a strong focus on the importance of entrepreneurship, family business, and leadership to family firms.

We also appreciate the contribution of Kellogg MBA students and alumni from family businesses around the world for their inspiration and insights over the past ten years. Also, special appreciation to the more than 400 participants in Kellogg's Governing the Family Business program for their stimulation and experience.

Our family business colleagues have shared ideas, and critical insights, and provided encouragement and support; we thank them all warmly for their contributions to this book. The Family Firm Institute and Family Business Network and all the consultants and advisors influence our thinking and are important contributors to the field of family business research and teaching.

We are very fortunate to have the support of Elin Williams, who worked on the final editing of the manuscript and contributed interviews with families, Fergal Byrne who provided early research support on the book, and Professor Lucia Tepla of INSEAD who made excellent comments on the final proof. We are also happy to be working again with Stephen Rutt and his very professional team at Palgrave Macmillan.

Most of all, we would like to thank the INSEAD and Kellogg students and families from around the world who shared their stories and experiences, taking us into their lives and businesses. Our goal was to highlight how business families successfully address their issues and challenges on both personal and professional levels. The families that attend our classes, programs, and conferences always talk about the importance of learning from other families and we hope that this book contributes to that goal.

RANDEL S. CARLOCK
JOHN L. WARD

Preface

Families are about caring and businesses are about money – making family business an unlikely formula for a successful partnership. Yet those are the facts, and family businesses around the world have found that parallel planning for these two often-conflicting systems is the key to family harmony and business success. *When Family Businesses are Best* is based on the parallel planning concepts first introduced five years ago in the book *Strategic Planning for the Family Business,* by the same authors. The new *Parallel Planning Process* is an improved version of a proven tool for aligning the family and business systems by linking values, vision, strategy, investment, and governance actions into a comprehensive family enterprise plan.

When Family Businesses Are Best is designed to be both rigorous and practical – explaining complex ideas with business-friendly frameworks and real-world examples. This book is written to help business families, and especially owners and non-executives, appreciate planning and governance concepts. It is about how successful family businesses work together, rather than providing a "how to plan" guide. The authors use interviews, research, and personal consulting experiences to develop case studies from around the world that demonstrate how successful business families turn family commitment into a competitive advantage that builds long-term value for the family, the business, and its stakeholders. The quotes highlighting the ideas and experiences of other family business owners and leaders are designed to help readers see the possibilities that exist for their own family businesses.

There are three universal challenges facing business families in the twenty-first century: first, addressing generational leadership and ownership transitions; second, engaging the family to ensure that its commitment becomes a competitive advantage; and third, aligning the family's investment of its financial and human capital with the business' strategy for value creation in an intensely competitive global economy. Complicating these efforts are continuous changes in the family and business systems caused by individual life cycle events, globalization, emerging and maturing markets and firms, business complexity, changing technology, and intense competition. These forces all threaten to disconnect the family and business systems resulting in conflicts and weak performance.

As the family grows and develops and the business becomes more successful, the family needs to be proactive in its planning and decision-making – if it envisages having a continued influence and contribution. The increased complexity in both the family and the business system demands effective planning tools and models. The *Parallel Planning Process* integrates five interrelated steps: agreeing on the family's shared values; crafting a family business vision; planning for family participation and business strategy; making capital investment – both financial and human; and governing the family and the business to ensure continued successful performance.

We argue that a lack of planning for the family is a serious threat to sustaining its members' commitment – probably the most important competitive advantage of family-controlled firms. The founder-entrepreneur's commitment of talent and money is a key factor that drives all aspects of the business' early success.

Unfortunately this global commitment naturally diminishes with each subsequent generation, as the family expands and a separation of management and ownership roles occurs. It is predictable, but often surprising to a family in the second or third generation, that it should face a new set of challenges: how to share ownership among a growing number of members; how to decide who will lead the business; how to define the rights and responsibilities of family owners. If the family has not planned and made decisions together, then every family or business issue has the potential to become a family conflict. On the other hand, if there are clear agreements and plans, on employment for example, then procedure and consistency, not personalities and power, become the drivers of family interactions.

The family's contribution is fundamental to sustaining the business' competitiveness and performance. If the family wants a growing business it needs to demonstrate commitment through active participation and investment. As the business family grows and matures, its members need to transmit values that support learning in each generation. The founder-entrepreneur demonstrated commitment to the business in every action, but this innate dedication is no longer possible by the third or fourth generation.

OUR FAMILY BUSINESS PARADIGM

Too often the mass media and even academic literature portray family business as a flawed model that needs to be improved (economics and management) or a pathology that needs to be healed (psychology and therapy). We believe otherwise. We see the members of business families, who share the same DNA, history, and core values, as having the potential to harness emotional connection to create social, emotional, and financial value. A family's emotional bonds, can, with good communication and careful planning, become a strategic advantage and a powerful tool for building and maintaining a significant social and business enterprise.

When Family Businesses Are Best reflects several beliefs about the nature of family business in the twenty-first century, born out of our experience of teaching and advising families around the world. First, families are complex systems facing continuous change and renegotiation of relationships because of life cycle transitions and dynamic business environments. Second, there are three proven tools for improving family functioning and business performance: communication, planning, and governance. Third, business families need to align the family and business in an integrated fashion, as in the *Parallel Planning Process*, in order to protect family harmony and grow the business. Fourth, families who share values, and especially a strong commitment to business ownership, have a powerful advantage over their competition. Fifth, family business is a dynamic system composed of many interrelated parts, so performance can be improved by making small changes in behavior anywhere in the system.

Family business success does not happen by accident but requires a shared vision of the family as important to the business' performance – and of the business as contributing to the family's goals. Business families need not implement every idea in this book. Instead they should take small steps that will create consistent positive changes in areas that they feel are important to them.

Each family business has its own unique challenges, of course, but when a family is committed to using its resources to exploit new opportunities then it can generate not only outstanding economic performance but also stronger bonds between family members. We are not naive enough to think that all family businesses can function at this level, but we equally do not believe that the Gucci model of family business pathology, pain, and desperation, for all its great drama, offers anything to help business families perform better or advances family business research and knowledge – apart from a model of how not to behave.[1] Nor does it reflect reality. We believe that the majority of business families are capable of improving their performance if they are given the thinking and tools to create new options. And our experience of working with families over the last two decades bears this out.

THE IMPROVED *PARALLEL PLANNING PROCESS*

Sound planning, based on values and vision, leads to an effective business strategy that exploits opportunities as well as to a family guided by thoughtful and fair agreements. The *Parallel Planning Process* coordinates these two often-conflicting strategic activities to align business demands with family expectations. The *Parallel Planning Process* is a platform for family communication and shared understanding between family members and management about critical factors for long-term business growth and family harmony.

Over the last five years we have discussed our planning processes with business audiences, MBA students, executive education participants, family clients, and professional colleagues, who have offered many helpful suggestions on how to improve its effectiveness. Listening to others helped us realize that our planning concepts had to be less academic and more practitioner friendly if we wanted this book to become a part of the business family's tool kit.

A Sudanese family executive on an INSEAD program articulated this challenge when he made the following comment about our previous book, *Strategic Planning for the Family Business*, which introduced the *Parallel Planning Process*: "The ideas are great but I had to read it three times to understand them. Can't you make it more business friendly?" Another frequently heard comment was, "The book is fantastic but too Western." The new book reflects our interpretations of these – and many other – suggestions from colleagues and practitioners about style, layout, and cultural breadth. We also decided to focus more on the family dimension because we have observed that most family firms have sound business strategies but do little planning for family issues. While all companies can improve their business thinking, unaddressed family issues – such as fairness, the boundaries between roles, shared decision-making, and protecting relationships – are often an obstacle to business growth and continuity.

THE AUDIENCE

We want *When Family Businesses are Best* to become a planning handbook for family businesses around the world. It offers business families a practical framework for addressing the major challenges of family businesses. The book also presents a global perspective on family firms in straightforward language, so is of value to readers from all cultures and countries.

As professors we know the challenge that undergraduate and MBA students face in exploring a topic like family business in the classroom setting. This book is multi-disciplinary because family business thinking crosses the functional organization of most business schools. We hope this book and its case studies will help the academic community teach the challenges of business families from many different learning perspectives. The book is also designed to support executive education for business families, because it offers a real perspective on both family and business topics with added academic rigor.

Advisors and consultants to business families are another important audience for this book. Our work with professional organizations such as the Family Firm Institute, which has developed training and certification courses for family and wealth advisors, has reinforced our awareness of this large professional group and of the relevance of our ideas to the very important work that they do.

A GLOBAL PHENOMENON

Family business is the predominant form of commercial organization around the world. It is a global phenomenon. Family businesses share very similar challenges and concerns no matter what part of the world they come from. At a recent family business workshop for senior family leaders the participants were asked to identify the "issues that keep them up at night." The list is below. Can you tell if it was written by business families from Africa, Asia, Asia Pacific, Europe, the Middle East, North America or South America?

- parental interference
- board membership/selection
- fairness in family dealings
- family communication
- dividends versus investment
- gender and cultural values
- inheritance and ownership
- family values and behavior
- business competence
- family participation
- family influence on decisions
- the role of advisors
- non-family executives
- ownership succession
- personal versus business needs.

Business families speak a shared *family business language* based on similar goals and experiences that allow them to consider the menu of ideas available and then select what is workable in their cultural and social context. Very seldom can you put a group of people from around the world in a classroom and, after just a few minutes, watch them share their successes, coach each other on their challenges, and most importantly, learn from each other on both personal and business issues. This insight is reflected in this new book. Moreover, studying business families across cultures provides a rich learning experience that challenges family members to think in different ways. Focusing on business families that are too similar means that many exciting new possibilities remain invisible.

Gender is an example of a topic that demonstrates our cross-cultural approach perfectly. Many of the best discussions we have heard about gender have been in Asia and the Middle East, where the overlap with business issues can be particularly complex. The West may talk a good game but men usually still dominate its boards and senior management teams. It would therefore be foolish to offer global guidelines. Our solution to culturally based issues is instead to offer globally applicable tools – like *Fair Process* – and examples of business families that have made them work in their own cultural setting.

A ROADMAP FOR OUR READERS

This book is separated into five parts that combine to provide a comprehensive approach to thinking about and planning for the future of a family business. The first part of the book starts with a review of the structural issues that challenge family businesses and then explains how the *Parallel Planning Process* addresses these challenges. The remaining four sections cover values and vision, strategy and investment, governance, and stewardship. Our intention is to offer a planning scheme that integrates human concerns, business planning, and investment decisions based on stewardship that supports a successful family enterprise. Success is measured as value creation for the family and all its stakeholders.

PART I: WHY GLOBAL BUSINESS FAMILIES NEED PLANNING

Chapter 1 explores the unique landscape shaped by the overlap of the family and business systems, family and business life cycle changes, and conflicting goals. The importance of planning in aligning the family and business and in developing strong family commitment is a central theme. We also stress how future generations need to plan in order to develop skills, knowledge, and behaviors that were intuitive to the founder. The Bancroft family and Dow Jones are discussed to show the consequences of avoiding strategic planning and of ineffective family and business governance.

Chapter 2 introduces the new *Parallel Planning Process* with its improved focus on five interrelated action steps: values, vision, strategy, investment, and governance. Cargill, the world's largest private family business, is used to demonstrate how the *Parallel Planning Process* has helped the Cargill and MacMillan families develop an entrepreneurial commitment that has maintained growth and continuity of family ownership.

PART II: CREATING HUMAN MEANING

Part II is an exploration of social issues, starting in Chapter 3 with a discussion of how family values and business culture create the basis for a family's planning and actions. The family vision then becomes the roadmap for the family's contribution to becoming a competitive advantage.

Chapter 4 considers how the family's vision is the basis for the family's relationship with the business and its stakeholders. Business families must share a vision that articulates the family willingness to invest the family's human and financial capital – as stewards of the family legacy.

PART III: STRATEGIES FOR FAMILY AND BUSINESS

Chapters 5 and 6 explore the strategic planning processes required to develop family leadership and ownership – and to craft a sound business plan that exploits the firm's strengths and opportunities.

Chapter 7 describes how the business planning process defines the firm's *Strategic Potential*, which is then matched with the family's commitment as a basis for making investment decisions. The chapter offers a *Family Business Investment Matrix* to help owners consider their investment decisions in a logical and structured manner.

PART IV: FAMILY AND BUSINESS GOVERNANCE

The two chapters in this section explore governance and the integration of family and business decision-making and accountability. Chapter 8 provides an overview of governance and examines how the board of directors is a partner with management and owners in strategy development, decision making, and accountability. Chapter 9 explores family governance, including family meetings, sound family agreements, and addressing conflict. Family and business governance are the critical factors in ensuring that the family and business plans are aligned and effectively implemented.

PART V: FAMILY ENTERPRISE STEWARDSHIP

The final chapter discusses how the family's stewardship of its enterprise supports the family's legacy. We use a French short story, "The man who planted trees," to demonstrate stewardship values and actions. We examine each of the five *Parallel Planning Process* steps and discuss how – when properly implemented –they help a family-owned enterprise to create value across a range of family activities. This short section is inherently about how a capable and entrepreneurial family team, who share values and a vision of where they are going, is the key to family enterprise growth and ownership continuity.

CONCLUDING THOUGHTS

We believe that the five action steps of the *Parallel Planning Process* offer a logical template for any business family engaged in planning at any stage of business or family development. The twenty-first century is a new era of global opportunity for human creativity – particularly for family businesses. We believe that the best professional practices of successful family enterprises can provide lessons for the entire business community. Business families have a competitive advantage when they align the planning processes for their families and businesses to make both more professional and mutually supportive. We know this advice may appear counter-intuitive but our experience shows that professionalizing the family –not just the business – supports harmony, trust, and stronger personal relationships.

This book reflects our values as teachers and advisors to business families, which include the importance of learning together. Family business is not about statistics and analysis, but rather it is about understanding the motivations and experiences of successful families – whose perspectives and experiences we share in each chapter. We hope that we have captured what business families and our colleagues have taught us. But most of all, we hope that our insights inspire a whole new set of families to go out and prove that family businesses are best.

RANDEL S. CARLOCK
PARIS AND SINGAPORE

JOHN L. WARD
CHICAGO

SEPTEMBER 2010

Part I

Why Global Business Families Need Planning

1 Why Family Businesses Struggle

Dysfunctional, prone to nepotism and family conflict, uninterested. This is how family businesses are often seen. Even in the business press, the family business model is regularly portrayed as outmoded or problematic. However, recent evidence shows that family firms tend to outperform their widely traded competitors. A research study in the *Journal of Finance* found that family businesses outperform public companies on key dimensions such as stock price and return on equity. The Credit Suisse Bank's global index shows that family firms have outperformed the MSCI World Index by 4.8 percent since January 2007.[1] How can this disparity be explained? Our work as researchers, teachers, and consultants suggests that family businesses can indeed be both the best and the worst: the best because they have some unique strengths (long-term vision, strong values, committed ownership); the worst, because they are more complex than other businesses, and they require more attention, better planning, and governance – which they do not always receive.

Typically, family businesses have sound strategies for their businesses, but planning for the families is mostly neglected or driven by conflicts that need to be resolved. Indeed, in our experience, many business families do not appreciate the value of planning, or are afraid of the emotional minefields that such planning may expose. Many fear that the process itself may raise questions that no amount of planning can resolve.

The central theme of *When Family Businesses are Best* is that high-performing business families need planning that provides rigor and consistency to drive their thinking, alignment and actions for both family and business. We call this *Parallel Planning* and advocate a process-driven approach. We argue that the best results come when a family work together to craft their own plans based on their unique situation and their family business goals.

But do families really need to plan? We think that the case of Farview Electronics offers a cautionary tale for planning skeptics. Back in the mid-1990s, this Hong Kong-based manufacturer of low-cost electronic components had been a nice little earner for the founding family for several decades – with little or no planning for the business, let alone the family. But complacency always comes at a cost.

FARVIEW ELECTRONICS TO BE SOLD?

At fiscal year end 1996, the Farview Electronics Company completed 30 consecutive years in the black since its founding.[2] The company motto was simple, "We produce low cost electronic components for everyone!" And the business strategy was even simpler: If it ain't broke, don't fix it! The two brothers who managed the family-owned Hong Kong firm – Lee and Charlie Tang – could be forgiven for their attitude. Their limited investment in capital expenditures for new products or equipment had enabled them and their two sisters to receive continually larger dividend payments for several years.

Things couldn't go on this way. And they didn't. June 2001 found the company looking back at five consecutive years of red ink, with the previous fiscal year the worst. During the 1990s the Tangs' sales shrank as many of their customers moved to China for lower-cost parts. Nor did it help when a competitor acquired a large parts distributor in Taiwan, threatening Farview's established sales channels in that market.

Charlie Tang, the 74-year-old chairman, says, "For 30 years, we were a profitable company, so nobody questioned the informal way things were done, and people had confidence in the family management." Charlie Tang continues:

> The problems really started three years ago when my older brother died and we split the business, and his two sons took ownership of the factory that their father had managed. My nephews, recognizing the changing market, started producing higher-margin components for manufacturers like HP and IBM. In the past I could have made it with one factory but now many of our old customers are reducing their number of suppliers – preferring to buy from companies that produce electronic sub-assemblies rather than just the component parts. Unfortunately it would require both plants working together to meet their needs.

Tang has not spoken to his nephews or their families for over two years.

Early in 2002, Tang persuaded his 33-year-old son, who was working as an executive for Intel in the United States, to return to Hong Kong and replace him as CEO. The first thing the younger Tang did was to cut costs and head count. The total number of employees went from 178 in mid-year to 125 by year-end, and crept back up to 150. For the fiscal year ending in June 2003, the company was marginally profitable.

Charlie Tang says:

> That was the result of cost cutting. Sales were actually down 28 percent, but that was planned as we exited lower-profit businesses. My son cut out a tremendous amount of fat from the overhead including two executive positions held by my sisters' sons-in-law – that really upset my sisters! The seriousness of the situation forced us to reduce the family dividend to help our cash flow; unfortunately the rest of the family doesn't understand why they are not getting more money from the business.

That, however, was just the start of the family conflict. Tang recently announced that he was seriously considering a purchase offer from a Hong Kong private equity fund that acquires distressed companies. The old Tang company would be merged into another manufacturer with all family ownership and employment eliminated. Tang's son, who is the current CEO, and his sister, who is vice president of finance and has worked at the firm for 16 years, are opposed to the sale but they currently own no voting stock.

The Tang family story exemplifies all the challenges that demand a more thoughtful and inclusive planning process for the family and business. The business is a mature organization in a highly competitive market with weak prospects for growth or profitability. The family is struggling as it attempts to meet the expectations of multiple generations and branches. It is also trying to cope all at once with the death of a founder, the sisters' role as non-employed owners, and the firing of the sisters' sons-in-law. Any one of these forces could prove damaging to the business or family relationships, but the combined impact seems to spell the end for both. It may be too late for Farview, but the *Parallel Planning Process* could have saved them, if only they had acted – and above all planned – earlier.

The *Parallel Planning* model involves five steps (or processes) driven by the family's values, because values shape vision, strategy, investment and governance (see Figure 1.1 overleaf). These five steps are the essence of the *Parallel Planning Process*. They provide focus and

Figure 1.1 *The five steps of the parallel planning process*

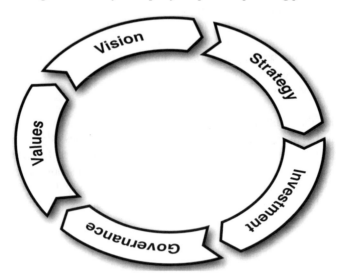

a unity of purpose, and align the family's commitment to the business with the business' potential to create value. In simple terms there are five actions for the family and five parallel actions for the business that, when completed with communication and shared thinking, create strong alignment of the two systems, focusing financial and human capital toward a shared and mutually supportive vision. We will describe the *Parallel Planning Process* extensively in the next chapter and discuss its specific applications throughout the book.

THE FAMILY BUSINESS CHALLENGE

Sigmund Freud observed that the intensity of family and work relationships is created by the conflict between *lieben und arbeiten* (love and work). He suggested that love and work are the main sources of self-esteem and pleasure in life, and that only when both are balanced do we achieve satisfaction.[3] So the two most important dimensions of our lives are connected in family businesses – failure or conflict in one will affect the other. The stakes are high.

Families and businesses are very different animals. Each system has different approaches to decision making, style of communication, and so on. While the norms of the business system may be easier to see and more standardized, the norms and operation of the family system are unique to each family, and often motivations and behaviors are hidden, less obvious. Yet the norms of the family system are deep and strong and can dominate the business system, causing all kinds of problems. Family members may, for example, feel automatically entitled to work in the business, just as they have automatic inclusion in the family. These individuals need to consider the business' demands and balance their feelings of entitlement with a larger vision of family and business success. The advantage of the *Parallel Planning Process* is that it forces the family to consider its values and vision, at the same time as its members make decisions about their relationships with the business.

There is an inherent tension between the needs and expectation of the family and those of the business. According to a 2008 Price-waterhouseCoopers survey, more than one-third of family businesses experience tension when considering the future business strategy. The study goes on to identify family member performance, decisions about working in the family business, failure to communicate decisions, and reinvestment versus dividends, as examples of conflicts between family expectations and business needs that create tension.[4] Careers are always a potential issue because most parents see their offspring as capable and entitled to their family's support. The parent's logic is simple: we own a family business that needs people and my child needs a job.

However, this logic fails when a family member expects a job but lacks the skills that the business needs. This can occur if the family has not properly planned a process for hiring its members or there is a lack of fairness in recruitment decisions. Either of these scenarios will create conflicts with possible consequences for the business and for family relationships. However, a simple family agreement would ensure that family members know the business' requirements, that the family perceives it is being treated fairly, and that the business seeks qualified employees.

The logical starting point is for the family to meet and clarify its values and then its future vision. As we will see in the next chapter, the family's values shape the vision statement, which determines what the business will become, and consequently its business strategy. If the vision is to remain a small, family-managed firm, competing in a local or regional market, then an open-door policy for family employment is possible. The employment criteria for family members in this business scenario are primarily interest, loyalty, and service, and family members can certainly fill the majority of the executive roles.

If, on the other hand, the vision involves aspirations for growth and perhaps global industry leadership, then the family must consider the business' needs for a large management team with the skills to craft and implement a more demanding business strategy. In this second scenario, the business will require a highly skilled management team, which could include qualified family and many non-family executives in key roles. As this very simple example shows, the *Parallel Planning Process* starts by clarifying values and then helps families to agree on a vision statement that drives planning to align family and business activities, thus ensuring the best possible family and business performance.

Family expectations and business demands are not always in conflict. Indeed it is a basic premise of this book that family businesses succeed best when the needs of both families and businesses are aligned. Yet, as we will demonstrate, there are many situations where the family makes an uninformed decision based on family goals, which can cause the business to suffer. Our experience with countless family businesses suggests that the needs and expectations of the two systems have to be balanced across five issues: control, capital, careers, connection, and culture (see Figure 1.2), and that business families need to communicate and plan to address these five pivotal variables.

Think about the Tangs again. They faced all five of the issues identified above. The business was struggling but there was uncertainty about who was in control: the senior Tang, his son the CEO, or his nephews operating their father's plant. Capital was a major issue because the dividends compete with the business' financial resources. Careers were a serious issue, with the sons-in-law being fired and the jobs of all the next generation under threat from the sale of the business. Connections between family members were strained across generations, between cousins, and even within the elder Tang's family. The final challenge of creating a family culture was perhaps the underlying reason for all the problems because it does not appear

Figure 1.2 *Globally five factors demand planning and governance to balance business demands and family expectations*

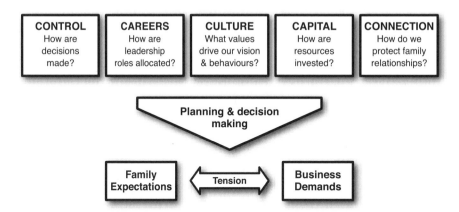

that family values were a part of the Tang family's thinking or considerations. What did they want the business to become? Was it just an economic entity or a family entitlement? Did it represent the Tang family heritage and their legacy?

If the family had practiced proper planning they would still have faced many of the same issues. Businesses and owners mature, older brothers die, family members want dividends, and the next generation wants careers. But, if no effort is made to plan and to align the family and the firm, any one of these issues can be fatal to the business and to the family. Family members who have planned together are in a position to coordinate their efforts and address challenges together instead of fighting among themselves. This is the major benefit of planning: it helps the family consider scenarios and options, and work together to develop a shared vision of the business, supported by strategies, investment, and governance.

We find it helpful for business families to understand the predictable tensions across the five fundamental issues of control, careers, culture, capital, and connection. The key is to ensure that the family and the firm have a planning system that aligns the decisions and actions of both systems around these issues. Although the respective needs and expectations of the two systems are unlikely to remain in perfect balance, the family and the business can work together to create plans and actions that are at least mutually supportive.

Control

How decisions are made is a central issue that needs to be negotiated for business families, especially as the business matures. Decision making is complex in a family business because of the different roles that family members play in the two systems. While the children are young and growing, the parents are at the top of the hierarchy, making the key decisions. Then, as the children mature and it becomes a family of adults, there is a shift to more shared decision making but with the parents still at the head of the family. Tension often develops when the younger generation takes charge of the business, as CEO and directors, but are still "under" their parents in terms of the family hierarchy. However, it is possible to get the balance right. Paddy McNeely, CEO of Meritex, a US warehousing and distribution company owned by his family, describes his father's role in the decision-making process: "He is generally pretty quiet. But we tend to be respectful to him and to the gift that he's given us. He's an influence, but doesn't exercise it too strongly. Let's just say that his voice is more equal than others – and rightly so!"

Careers

Our careers and families, "work and love" in Freud's terms, are the critical factors in a meaningful human life. Normally career choice is an individual decision for a young adult. In the early stages of a family business, however, family members often work there without concern for job description or qualifications. As the business grows and professionalizes and the number of family members with potential career interest in it expands, status, qualifications, and performance become the basis for employment decisions. Luay Abu-Ghazaleh, vice chairman of the Talal Abu-Ghazaleh Organization, the largest professional services group in the Middle East, explains how careers are managed in his family business:

> As family members, all of the next generation will be eligible for careers in the business. But there are set criteria: they have to obtain a related university education and spend at least two years working outside the business, before joining at a level appropriate to their skills and experience and – provided all goes well – working their way up.

Culture

Every family has a set of values or a sense of "how the family believes things should be done" – however well defined and articulated. To a greater or lesser degree, these values shape the culture of a family business. They also have a powerful impact on the success of the business. Positive values like entrepreneurship and integrity are the backbone of many successful family businesses. Ineffective values, like secrecy and unwillingness to trust, have a negative impact. Families need to be aware of their own values and the impact that they have on their business performance. Tim Wates, a fourth-generation owner and family leader, explains the thinking of the Wates Group, one of the largest privately owned construction and development companies in the United Kingdom: "Our family enterprise values are written down: unity, enterprise, sustainability, integrity, and leadership. They could be seen as rather male and hard-edged. But they work for us."

Capital

There are two dimensions to a family business' investment: financial and human capital. We will discuss the investment of the family's human capital in detail throughout the book. Decisions about what to do with the financial capital created by business success are fundamental to every family business. How much should be allocated to dividends versus reinvested in the business is one key question. How to reward management for its contribution to business performance is another. At a simple level there seems to be a tension between the financial needs of the family and those of the business. Certainly, many successful family businesses have a strong commitment to reinvesting a high percentage of the profits in the business to support future growth. Also there can also be serious issues about how to allocate shares in the company, who can be owners, and how to redeem shares to create liquidity if an owner wants to sell. Mohammed Abduljawad, chairman and CEO of a large transportation group in Saudi Arabia, illustrates the point:

> One of the important ownership steps for our family was a clear exit strategy for owners wanting to sell their stock. When it is clear how family members exit it encourages people to stay. Our goal is to ensure that ownership issues don't hinder the business.

Connection

Many members of business families are keen to maintain strong and enduring family relationships and connections. In the earliest stages of a family business' development, the entrepreneur usually plays a central role in the family. Family relationships are often anchored around the business, and family members have relationships with each other through the founder and the business. These strong and durable connections create an extra sense of family, and serve as the glue that holds the family together. Bill Fisher, former president of GAP International and a current board member, captures the challenges of maintaining connection with the business: "Growing up, it was always a topic at dinner. But the next generation doesn't live it like we did. That means part of my role is to be a storyteller for my children." As families and businesses grow and mature, they need to explore how planned and structured family activities, rather than the business, can become the new glue that holds them together.

Differing family and business goals

Widely traded or public companies are focused primarily on financial goals, such as growing profits or increasing shareholder value through a higher stock price. While all family businesses want strong financial performance from their businesses, there are many other dimensions by which families measure performance. Some may, for example, attach more importance to social responsibility and therefore protect jobs with a no-layoff policy. For example Jerónimo Martins, a Portuguese food distribution company, declared it "would sack employees only as a last resort after cutting salaries, bonuses, investment and dividends."[5] These families choose to hold on to employees during an economic downturn because they want to protect them or retain an investment in the community that cannot be justified in purely financial terms.

Clearly agreed business goals are necessary to focus the family's energy and commitment; when unclear or diverging, they can be a source of conflict and struggle for both family and business. Ignoring some of the family's goals, for whatever reason, inevitably weakens the family's commitment to the business. Family businesses that over-emphasize business goals, at the expense of the family's aspirations and vision, often end up with uncommitted family members who do not relate to each other and psychologically compete with the business. Similarly families that prioritize the needs of the family over those of the business can weaken the business' competitive position.

Our work with business families suggests that there are four key sets of goals that matter to business families (see Figure 1.3). These goals are expressed differently across cultures but represent the family's attempt to work together to create meaning beyond the simple economic gain that is the basis for most business relationships.

Figure 1.3 *Hierarchy of family business goals*

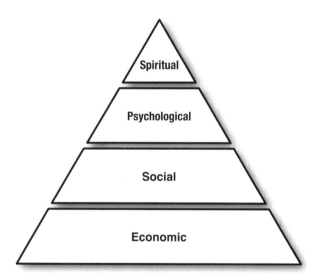

- *Economic*: Wealth creation and preservation is about growing and sustaining the family's wealth.
- *Social*: Symbolic responsibilities and business reputation are important for many families. They might see themselves as representing the interests of their community, the larger business community, or even their nation. These families place great significance on using their economic power and prestige to contribute to society as a whole.
- *Psychological*: Individual talent development and emotional wellbeing represent the family's attempt to use its business activities

as a platform for developing its members' skills and creating opportunities for them to experience professional success.

■ *Spiritual*: The family seeks to create deeper personal or collective meaning in their lives. Typically these goals are expressed through religious commitment or service to others with no business connections.

Many of these softer non-financial goals can be difficult to evaluate in a clear systematic manner. Measuring profits is pretty straightforward, but how do you set and measure social goals for the family? How do you express a trade-off between a family's social and financial goals – even assuming there is a clear consensus within the family about their relative priority? Conflict can occur when family members are not clear about what goals are being pursued or when differences in priorities are not communicated as a part of the family's planning and governance processes.

As the ownership group expands over time, family goals and their relative importance inevitably change. The founder-entrepreneur may remain focused primarily on business growth, relentlessly pushing the business to new levels, while some members of the next generation could be more concerned about career opportunities, availability of capital to spend, or wealth protection. The multi-generation family needs to confirm its shared, often multifaceted, values – and then agree on a vision that drives strategic thinking and planning for the family and business.

Family and business life cycle transitions

Life cycle change is a given in any discussions of humans or the organizations they create. Families are directly influenced by life events that shape the nature and character of relationships and interactions.[6] Children growing up, marriages, births, divorces, and deaths alter the structure of the family and require the negotiation of new relationships. Life cycle events, such as a next-generation family member finishing university and asking for a job in the family firm, often trigger challenges in the family business system. The tried and tested relationship of three siblings managing and owning a business together is suddenly jeopardized when their children join the organization. Problems often arise from transitions or when family members fail to renegotiate their relationships in the light of such changes. A son or daughter who has completed an MBA and worked successfully elsewhere expects to be treated like an adult on joining the family firm. If not, there will be frustration, or worse, resentment and conflict.

Human life follows a predictable pattern over an average of 70 to 80 years. The cycle goes from birth, through growth and development, to the highly productive early to mid-adult years, and then a steady period in late adulthood (see Figure 1.4). These events play out in the family business, in terms of both management and ownership changes. In businesses, managers and owners have the most direct influence during their early and mid-adult years, from around age 35 until they shift focus in their sixties or seventies.[7]

The mid-adult years reflect a combination of experience, endurance, and personal motivation that enable individuals to create and drive businesses. Sooner or later new interests, the desire to empower the next generation, or perhaps declining health will mean that management and ownership responsibilities are transferred. Another pressure is that children, cousins, and grandchildren may all want careers as leaders in the business. Successions are directly influenced by both individual and

Figure 1.4 *The human life cycle and biological imperative*

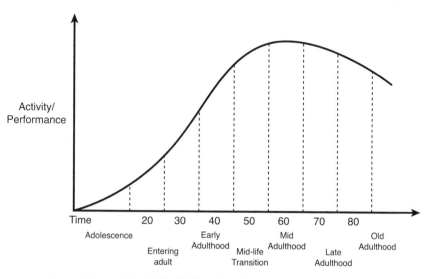

Source: Erikson, E. H. (1950) *Childhood and Society.* New York: W.W. Norton.

family life events. The death of the chairperson and largest shareholder, for example, reverberates throughout the family and the business.

Transferring ownership and control between generations is one of the biggest challenges facing family businesses. In discussing the challenges to family businesses a recent *Economist* article points out that,

> the alignment of ownership and management, can become a weakness when control passes to the next generation. "Sometimes they are arrogant, sometimes they are naïve, sometimes they are really very good, but they are never the original entrepreneurs," according to Volker Beissenhirtz of the German law firm Schultze & Braun.[8]

Family businesses must cope with business-related life cycle issues while simultaneously working on successions driven by the human life cycle. Businesses face life cycle challenges as they and their industries mature. The life cycle diagram (see Figure 1.5) shows the interaction of family as well as business life cycle forces, influencing the development of four typically occurring ownership configurations (Owner-Manager, Sibling Partnership, Cousin Collaboration, and Family Enterprise).[9] It is nevertheless possible for families to skip ownership phases or revert to an earlier phase, such as Owner-Manager, if there are no heirs or there is a stock buyback.

These challenges are not unique to a particular family enterprise. Rather, they are related to predictable transitions that occur as both families and businesses grow and mature. Yet all too often these issues are not planned for in a systematic or coherent way. Each generation may be making different assumptions regarding future desires and intentions. A young organization while making the transition to a Sibling Partnership requires different strategies and tactics than a mature business in the Family Enterprise stage. None of these happen automatically, and they require thoughtful strategies and governance.

Understanding how life cycle influences family businesses is a valuable insight and strongly supports family business planning. The overlapping relations and roles mean that individual and family life events have a direct impact on the business. When the CEO of a publicly traded company retires, the selection of a new CEO is a rational process based on finding the most qualified candidate. Replacing the oldest brother as CEO in a family business is never a totally rational

Figure 1.5 *Family ownership is influenced by individual, family, and business life cycle transitions*

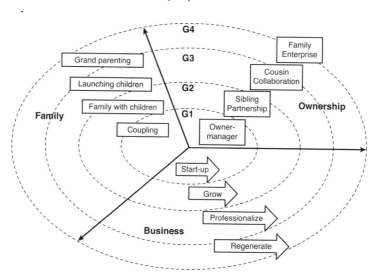

Adapted from: Sigelman, C.K. and Shaffer, D.R. (1991) *Life-Span Development.* Belmont, California: Brooks/Cole Publishing; Eggers, J.H., Leahy, K.T. and Churchill, N.C. (1978) *The Season of a Man's Life.* New York: Balantine Book; 'Stages of small business growth revisited: insights into growth path and leadership/management skills in low and high growth companies', in Bygrave, W. D., Birely, S., Churchill, N. C., Gatewood, E., Hoy, F., and Wetzel W. E. (eds) (1994) *Frontiers of Entrepreneurship Research.* Boston, Mass.: Babson College.

process, especially when the potential successors are younger relatives. Sibling rivalry, hidden agendas, disagreements between generations or branches, and parent–child conflicts may all play a role. It is important to consider ownership succession because it is ownership that defines a multi-generation family business. Executive succession, while not always simple, at least has the marketplace to guide it.

The separation of ownership and management roles

Family businesses begin with an owner-manager, partners or a husband and wife (see Figure 1.6). During the Owner-Manager stage these two critical roles are fully aligned because one person fills the management and ownership roles. Even if the founders are partners or a couple the

Figure 1.6   *The separation of management and ownership roles*

	Owner- manager	Sibling Partnership	Cousin Collaboration	Family Enterprise
G1	■	■		
G2		○●●	●○●●	●●○
G3			△△△▲▲△	△▲△▲▲△
G4				△△▲▲△◮

■ = Family owner-employees

▨ = Family owners

☐ = Family members

alignment is very tight. In this phase the priority is survival and growth of the business.

The founder's children join the family business and trigger the Sibling Partnership stage, representing an increase in the number of family members and the potential for different goals and expectations. During this stage the business faces its first separation of ownership and management roles, as some siblings may be owner-managers while others are just owners. The sibling generation tends to focus on building the business and professionalizing management of the firm. The siblings' challenge is to bring in their own children (the cousins) and to consider new models of planning and governance. Note that in Figure 1.6 there are three symbols shaded black, representing family owner-employees, a gray symbol representing a family owners who do not work in the firm and white for family members without ownership or employment connections. As the family moves to generations three and four typically the percentage of owner-employees decreases.

Some families consciously decide to exclude family members from employment in the business in order to support a professionally managed organization or reduce family conflicts. Tony Echavarria, former president of his family council, describes how Corona, his family's business in Colombia operates:

We have a policy that none of the family can work in the business – except for training roles or short-term posts. They may only participate at a policy level, as part of the corporate, foundation or family boards, and as members of the Family Assembly. This policy came straight from the second generation. At that point they withdrew and gave the business over to professional management. So far some of the fourth generation have questioned it, but there has been no change.

Daniel Echavarria, a Corona board member from the fourth generation, chair of the family's foundation council and Tony's second cousin, supports the policy:

> I feel comfortable that we're not allowed to work in the business. It's always been the status quo. But in the long term, as the shareholdings get diluted, we may risk losing the family's knowledge and commitment to the business. We have to be careful.

The Cousin Collaboration stage brings an expanded number of family members, who may have had limited experience of the founder and business. If their parents did not work for the business, it may not even have been the major topic of conversation as they were growing up. The business' demand for professional leadership also requires that next-generation family members have education and training for business careers. The further separation of management and ownership roles makes decision making and communication both more important and more challenging. Accountability for performance, decisions on strategy, investment, and family participation, which were once the responsibility of a small group of employed family members, are now shared among a family or possibly non-family management team, the board of directors, the owners, and a larger family group. This expansion of the family means that decision making needs to be formalized for these groups and its relationship with governance clarified.

The last phase of ownership is the Family Enterprise stage, which represents another shift in planning and governance as the business goes public and the family expands its attention to new activities such as a family office for investments or family foundation for charitable activities. Cargill, the world's largest agri-business, is an example of a multi-generational family enterprise. A non-family CEO leads the business, with family participating only as investing owners and on the board of directors. The family office, Waycrosse, provides a wide range of investment and other services to the family, and the Cargill Foundation supports education and research. The ownership group influence the business as investors, and the role of governance becomes a critical factor in maintaining family influence and ensuring management accountability for both the business and family activities.

The impact of the family as owners is often overlooked because shareholders often see ownership as of secondary importance to management. Claude Janssen, honorary chair of INSEAD and chair of the school's International Council, questions this thinking:

> The biggest challenge for family businesses in the twenty-first century is leadership succession and not necessarily in terms of the CEO. Without strong family leadership as committed owners and directors, family businesses will disappear. This has been the issue "forever" when you have a family as the major stakeholder.

Indeed, while executive roles are important, the typical executive will serve less than ten years as CEO, whereas an owner may serve many decades. Owners influence strategy and management formally, when they elect the board of directors and express their vision and goals, and informally in designating and training the next generation of owners. The latter informal influence often sets the course of family leadership and participation for many generations to come.

THE COMPETITIVE ADVANTAGE OF A COMMITTED BUSINESS FAMILY

Many experts believe entrepreneurship is a "necessary condition for family firm continuity."[10] At the earliest stages of a family business, this entrepreneurial commitment is a given. The entrepreneurs who create family business are first and foremost committed to making their business venture a success. The founder's "global" commitment of his or her creativity, business talents, and assets shapes all aspects of the new firm's culture and strategy. Unfortunately conflicts between the family and business systems, life cycle changes, and the separation of management and ownership roles, all discussed above, may weaken the commitment of the subsequent generations over time. As the family business grows and matures, ownership and management, once concentrated in the hands of the owner-manager, get distributed and dissipated across a wider array of individuals. As ownership spreads to individuals with different life experiences, values, and levels of business understanding, there is a danger of the family losing its coherence, focus, and commitment to owning the business. The larger number of family members also presents problems for achieving clarity, consensus, and agreement.

To succeed, business families need to plan to renew commitment with each succeeding generation, a commitment that is different in form but provides the same intention to grow and sustain the business as the founder offered. Unless the family works to ensure a broadly shared commitment to investing both their financial and human capital in the business, family ownership will lack impact and focus. We argue that families need to align their commitment with the demands of the business – and that this is a fundamental planning and decision-making activity at the heart of the *Parallel Planning Process*. For example, if the business has the opportunity to make a significant acquisition that could strengthen its market position, the family may need to be willing to forgo dividends or significant redemption freedom to fund this purchase. The management's main goal within the *Parallel Planning Process* is to strengthen the firm's competitive position and generate returns for the shareholders. The main goal for the family, as owners, should be to focus on maximizing their commitment over time. If a family cannot sustain its commitment it should explore plans to divest itself of the business at a good price.

Family commitment is essential if a business is to survive for multiple generations. It is a fact that families that have made the commitment to stewardship for the business, much like the founder did through his or her personal investment, stay in control longer. For entrepreneurs and second generation owner-managers, life is relatively simple: they are totally committed to their businesses socially, psychologically, and financially. They have a personal engagement with the business because it gives them financial and psychological rewards. This may not be the case for other members of the family, particularly in later generations, where the connections between family and business, and indeed between members of the family, are weaker. Here families will benefit from proactively integrating their financial and human investment strategies into their planning process. The *Parallel Planning Process* is designed to do this.

In simple terms the task is: how to create more committed families and thus prevent the succession of generations from undermining the success and performance of the business. This is one of the key themes of this book. Or, in more positive terms, how do we make sure that family ownership is a competitive advantage for the business? Family education and communication have a key role to play here. The senior generation must expose the next generation to the family business in order to help them consider how their talents and energy could enable them to be the business' future leaders and owners. The next generation needs to understand responsible ownership: the trade-offs between short-term personal rewards (dividends) and long-term family business success. A committed next generation of family owners is essential to the success of the family business' financial and strategic performance. In Chapter 5 we will look at this vital question in more detail.

Just as ownership and commitment evolve over generations, so must the nature of family members' entrepreneurship. This is an important but rarely understood phenomenon. Because family businesses professionalize as they grow, succeeding generations need to express their commitment and entrepreneurial talents through new activities, such as developing family and business visions and stewardship, as well as an expanded scope of topics including wealth and investment management, philanthropy, governance, unifying an expanded ownership group, sustaining family harmony, and supporting a larger community of stakeholders. Much of this spills into the domain of creating a family enterprise rather than the more narrow definition of a family business as an operating business. We believe that the family can best maintain and drive its commitment by undertaking new activities, like a family foundation or family office, that create value for the family beyond the core operating business.

The benefits of the *Parallel Planning Process*

As we have seen, families face significant challenges in maintaining family ownership across generations. Continued family ownership and business performance is not sustainable without communication and planning: families need a systematic framework for thinking about the future strategy of their families and of their businesses. Unfortunately recent research by PricewaterhouseCoopers shows that this is not happening:

> Only 50% of respondents said they had chosen a successor, and a significant percentage (44%) do not have in place a succession plan for key senior roles. Furthermore, it can take years to create an appropriate new holding structure for a family business, which increases the uncertainty about the future, and can jeopardize a company's earnings or even threaten its existence. If the owners should die prematurely without a solid succession plan in place, a host of stakeholders could be affected.[11]

This report suggests that business families need to spend more time planning.

We developed the *Parallel Planning Process* to provide family businesses with a structured planning approach that explicitly recognizes the five structural issues of control, capital, careers, connections, and culture, and the critical importance of maintaining family commitment over time. The *Parallel Planning Process* also provides a platform to support communication among family members, owners, and management about the essential factors for long-term business success and sustainable family harmony. Mikhail Kassam, a second-generation family executive from Midas Safety, a Canadian manufacturer and supplier of safety gloves, explains:

> Communication is a key ingredient in managing change and learning new behaviors – and all families must renegotiate their roles and structures as the family grows and matures. Family businesses need to reach a higher level of communication, to bring out the unspoken issues. What about the girls? Do we have the right leadership skills? What about the next generation? It's the things that remain unspoken that are the dangers in business – especially a family business.

As we have seen, family commitment is vital to family business success. In the most successful family businesses, owning families are willing to invest their talents, time, and financial resources in the business – and provide it with a powerful competitive advantage.

The *Parallel Planning Process* helps families do this explicitly by helping them think about how to use their talent, interest, and capital to support the business' growth over years and generations. Failure to maintain the family's commitment to its business can have disastrous consequences.

A family's commitment to ownership boils down to willingness to invest or risk its financial capital as well as its talent. We suggest that commitment is measured in economic terms by the family's reinvestment or disinvestment rate – including decisions about how to use earnings and cash flow, and whether to add new capital or take larger dividends. In effect the family's decisions about investment and future ownership are the final approval of the management's business strategy and a direct translation of the family's level of commitment. We address these decisions in detail in Chapter 4.

Families often continue to reinvest in their family business more or less out of habit – without considering their own level of commitment or the firm's potential to create value. Supporting a business that your family founded may appear to be responsible and prudent. Unfortunately this is not always a formula for creating wealth or family harmony. This is particularly true when the family are no longer able or willing to act as responsible owners. So what happens when a business family fails to make the necessary ownership commitment?

THE LACK OF A *PARALLEL PLANNING PROCESS*: THE BANCROFT FAMILY STORY[12]

It was one of the most colorful takeover battles in recent corporate history, pitching Rupert Murdoch, arguably the world's most powerful media tycoon, against the secretive Bancroft family, whose entrepreneurial ancestors, founders of Dow Jones, the publisher of the *Wall Street Journal* and *Barrons*, were early innovators in US financial journalism. Murdoch's takeover bid for the ailing company put the spotlight on the Bancrofts, as the family, in the words of one commentator, "flagellated itself" over whether to sell the *Wall Street Journal*. First the Bancrofts rejected Murdoch's offer out of hand, then they agreed to meet with him. Next Christopher Bancroft, a board member and trustee, decided to boycott a key family meeting; Leslie Hill, a family board member, did a volte-face, and refused to take a phone call from Rupert Murdoch, after initially agreeing to; and another family member resigned as trustee before the vote. Finally, in July 2007, the family agreed to sell the business.

There was no doubt Dow Jones was vulnerable. By the 1990s, the *Wall Street Journal* remained a small newspaper company – its market capitalization was only $3.2 billion – almost entirely focused on financial and business news. The Bancroft family had taken a hands-off approach, delegating control of the company to non-family management for the previous 30 years. Unfortunately the managers were first and foremost journalists, not business strategists. Their narrow focus resulted in Dow Jones' failure to pursue several significant opportunities in the financial information market that other family businesses or entrepreneurs exploited.

For example, Bloomberg L.P., which provides real-time financial information to investment professionals, created a new desktop market for the very information that had been printed by the *Wall Street Journal*. In contrast, another publishing family, the Canadian-based Thomson family, repositioned its business from small, local newspapers to become a global legal and business publisher. The Thomsons recently acquired Reuters and are now one of the largest business news services in the world. Finally, Pearson Publishing in the United Kingdom, which publishes the *Financial Times* (*FT*) as a British competitor to the *Wall Street Journal,* has expanded globally, making the *FT* a market leader in many parts of the world.

Dow Jones lasted as a family company for over 100 years but the family's failure to act on new market opportunities was a real value killer. The root of the problem was the Bancrofts' stewardship of the family business. No member of the Bancroft family had worked in senior management in Dow Jones in recent years. The various executives had enjoyed the wholehearted and largely unquestioning support of Jane B. Cook, 77, at the time the last surviving member of the third generation and the largest single shareholder. "The company has always been successfully run by newspapermen," she said. "There is a feeling these men have been tremendous assets to Dow Jones." While the Bancroft family had seats on the board, they were seen as little more than rubber stampers for management decisions.

Not only did the family fail to invest its human capital in the business; it also provided little financial support. Dow Jones had been good to Bancroft family members, who had taken large dividends from the business for decades. Indeed, in some years dividends had exceeded the company's profits – and just prior to approving the sale of Dow Jones to News Corp., the family had doubled the dividend it took from the company. All this capital depletion undoubtedly helped undermine the company's competitive position.

The Bancroft family rarely met to discuss the family business. When they did, the meetings were often run by one of the trustees. Moreover, the family had a largely unquestioning attitude towards management: for any Bancroft to question or criticize the way Dow Jones was run – even amongst other family members – was seen as an act of disloyalty. According to one of them, Crawford Hill, as they moved into the 1990s,

> to attempt to raise serious questions about management, strategy, the family's role as owners, as anything other than strong supporters of management, and to question the role of family directors, was to be branded a dissident.

At the time of the sale, a generational rift was apparent. The younger Bancroft family members realized the need either to sell the business or to support it actively and fund a reformulation of the strategy into new markets such as financial information. The senior family members defined their "commitment" as protecting journalistic integrity, rather than ensuring the competitiveness and economic viability of the firm or investing their money and talent in the business. As a result of a lack of family consensus on investment and ownership, Dow Jones was sold for less than its value ten years earlier – to a competitor the family could not abide for his journalistic and commercial practices.

In the final days before the sale of the company, Crawford Hill identified the root of the problems in an email to his family: "Our real legacy was an inherited lack of awareness as to what it takes to nurture and pass on an effective legacy, about what is really required to be responsible, engaged and active owners of a family business." The family's relationship with Dow Jones "was completely taken for granted," he continued, as was the whole question of responsible ownership:

> Such things can never be taken for granted – they must be actively nurtured, cultivated, questioned, tested and honed. That has not happened in our family in any meaningful way ... there has absolutely never existed any kind of family-wide/cross-branch culture of teaching what it means to be an active, engaged owner and, more crucially, a family director.

The story of the Bancroft family is an example of a failed legacy. The Bancrofts' ownership control should have provided them with significant influence on business strategy and financial performance. But instead of being governing owners they abdicated responsibility to the firm's management, a problem often seen in third-generation family businesses that have failed to plan and work together. After the Bancrofts sold the business to Rupert Murdoch one of them observed, "Had things been run differently, we might own a $50 billion business today not a $3.5 [billion] or even $5 billion business."[13]

WHEN FAMILY BUSINESSES ARE BEST

- The entrepreneurial family must develop family plans and business strategies to grow and sustain the business.
- Planning balances the inherent tension between the business' demands for funding and talent and the family's expectations for dividends and careers.
- Family and business leadership must plan succession based on the predictable life cycles that generate transitions and change.
- Building and sustaining family commitment is essential to the family becoming a competitive advantage to the business.

2 Making the Parallel Family and Business Planning Process Work

All organizations need planning to survive, grow, and sustain themselves. Businesses are forced to plan by competitive pressures, customers, suppliers, taxes, banks, joint ventures, or acquisitions. Businesses can plan reactively by making changes based on competition, adaptively by making changes based on the market or environment, or strategically by anticipating competitive and environmental forces. All businesses have some form of planning whether it is formally documented and implemented, or informal and reactive on a day-to-day basis. Planning is recognized as an important driver of business success.

The external forces that drive business planning do not encourage planning for the business family. Founders are business focused and typically do not see the need for family planning, especially their children's participation. It is assumed and natural. The second generation (or Sibling Partnership) anticipates its children joining with some planning. Formal planning is usually triggered when the third generation (or Cousin Collaboration) get involved, joining the business as employees and potential owners. Third-generation business families without planning processes lack the tools to manage a family that is growing larger and more complex. By this phase the family faces very specific challenges about:

- family employment and compensation
- career planning and succession
- ownership transfers
- dividend versus reinvestment
- shared decision making across generations.

One of the most serious challenges facing business families is that their businesses may have excellent, well-crafted plans but the family may never have discussed issues like succession or even day-to-day matters like family employment and compensation. Often business families will have no specific plans regarding family careers, ownership, or decision making until a conflict or crisis triggers a response. Without planning, problems arise. Disgruntled family owners bring up unanswered questions with the CEO at family social gatherings; unhappy family employees discuss family issues at board meetings. There are many reasons for this planning disconnect – including the significant difference in planning for a business versus planning for a family (see Table 2.1).

Multi-generational business families need aligned planning and decision-making processes to ensure performance and protect both family and business from needless conflict. It is also important to plan because the family's participation and leadership are, when the family's role is fully understood and clearly focused, a competitive advantage. However, many obstacles can get in the way, especially in planning for succession and ownership roles. In some cultures simply discussing succession or ownership is perceived as inappropriate. And in all cultures senior family leaders may resist planning for succession because they view it as a threat to their leadership roles, choosing instead to delay the process because the next generation is "not ready" or the issues are "too controversial and emotionally risky." Family executives may also resist organizing family meetings for fear of family interference with the business or losing control over the decision-making process.

Table 2.1 *Business versus family planning*

Behavior	Business planning	Family planning
Style	Formal	Informal
Timing	Annual	Generational
Performance	Financial	Emotional
Authority	Management	Family
Information	Private	Shared

Some senior family members may feel that exploring family topics interferes with what should be a natural process. Any formal planning process requires that independent-minded business leaders share decisions – and private financial statements – with others in the family and company. Business families risk being hurt by family misunderstandings, unprepared family members, or a next generation's unclear interests, if there is no reliable planning process. Identifying family values as a part of that process will enable the family to stimulate ideas for actions, which will help overcome the obstacles and resistance discussed above.

The best way to show the *Parallel Planning Process* in action is to analyze a large family business that has used an aligned planning process for the family and business for many years. Cargill, one of the world's largest multi-generation family businesses, illustrates the power of parallel planning to avert family conflicts, protect against business stagnation and strengthen shareholder commitment.

CARGILL: FROM CONFLICT TO COMPETITIVE ADVANTAGE

The Cargills and their in-laws the MacMillans have owned the world's largest agribusinesses for over 100 years, but it is a family history filled with conflicts and recriminations.[1] The business was founded by the Cargill family, which remained in control until the early 1900s, when a son-in-law from the MacMillan family became the CEO and his family the majority shareholder. This difficult ownership transition to an in-law and the subsequent loss of Cargill family control generated strong resentment between the two family branches. Many Cargill family members believed that their family business had been "stolen" from them, while the MacMillans felt unappreciated despite having "saved" the business from financial ruin.

The resulting animosity between the two families did serve one useful purpose. It focused both families' attention on building a shared vision based on their core values of entrepreneurship, fair play, and a commitment to long-term family ownership. Early on, the families began planning for the business and family to ensure that the business was protected from family strife and that professional management roles were earned based on qualification and performance. Family members competed with non-family executives for promotions, and often the non-family members won. A global growth strategy, based on low dividends and high investment, was implemented. Cargill far-sightedly invested in a state-of-the-art communications system and was an early user of computer technologies, giving it a significant competitive advantage in trading commodities or reacting to volatile markets.

Cargill's executive leaders have demonstrated their ability to maintain core values while changing the nature of the organization. They have always reflected a strong belief in "growing their own" top executives; in fact, all seven of Cargill's top executives have worked at the company for 30 years or more. Gregory Page, currently Cargill's (non-family) CEO, joined right after completing his university degree.

On the other hand, Cargill's ability to change its business strategy was reflected in the company's recent move from commodities to higher value-added activities. "It was clear in the late 1990s that the business model of the company for effective trade and processing was breaking down," said finance director Bob Lumpkins. "There was consolidation of our customers. Our offering wasn't very differentiated. We were up against focused competitors and our cost structure was too high."[2] In mid-1998 a team was created to set the direction until 2010. The review – dubbed "Strategic Intent" – involved considering four strategies, from reinvention as a volume supplier to focusing on specialty ingredients and consumer branding.

As Whitney MacMillan, the last family CEO, said shortly before his retirement, "As a company, we have believed in the same family values for 125 years, even though we have changed the business every five years." The link between this changing business strategy and sound planning for the family was evident in several innovations: the five board seats reserved for family directors (with five for independents and five for management); regular family meetings; and a strong family council. Cargill even organized a stock buyback to purchase shares from family members who no longer felt a commitment to the business and wanted to exit as owners, or needed some personal liquidity to continue their commitment. The stock was then sold to an employee ownership trust, making the Cargill Employee Stock Ownership one of the largest voting blocks – not a bad way to build employee commitment.

Perhaps the most important innovations are in family education and training. Waycrosse, the Cargill family office, handles training and education, as well as a wide range of family matters, such as financial planning, tax, and estate planning. A key goal is to keep family members who are not working in the business engaged with Cargill and with the family itself – to maintain the family connection. To achieve this, Waycrosse organizes education programs, summer family meetings, plant tours, shareholder meetings, and family task forces. The mandate of one task force, for example, the Family Connections and Education Task Force, is to "encourage education for the next generation as well as maintenance of that family glue."[3]

In short, the *Parallel Planning Process* at Cargill meant that, despite inter-family conflicts, the business was protected from family interference and was able to perform effectively. And the family glue was strengthened to support the business through its major changes in management and strategy. Greg Page, CEO of Cargill says it best: "The number of times I have been called by a family member to compare this year to last year is seldom."

As the Cargill case demonstrates, business planning is important, but it is planning for the family that sustains multi-generational ownership. It is also the latter kind of planning that presents the biggest challenges because of emotions, differences in talent and motivation, and family relationships. Business interactions are professional and temporal, meaning that plans require clarity and a relatively short time frame; family relationships, in contrast, are emotional and last forever. Planning is also typically not a part of the family's experiences; founders do not need or want formal structures or processes, and the Sibling Partnership generation adapts this informal style, working on a personal individual-to-individual, issue-to-issue basis. Consequently, in most successful first and second-generation firms there is a limited amount of formal planning for the family because an informal and reactive model has always worked well enough.

THE BENEFITS OF PARALLEL FAMILY AND BUSINESS PLANNING

In Chapter 1, we explored some of the particular structural challenges that make family businesses so complex, challenges that require family businesses to engage in a parallel process that takes into account the expectations of the family and the needs of the business. Indeed, the primary benefit of the *Parallel Planning Process* is that it aligns family and business plans so that they can mutually support each other's needs and goals, rather than work against each other's interests. For example, business strategies need to be considered in the context of the family's values and financial expectations. If, for example, the family values wealth creation, to continue with a low-profit business strategy would not meet the family's needs.

Families are organizations, and as they grow in size and complexity, they need a planning process to coordinate thinking, participation, and action. A well-organized family reduces the opportunities for conflict and therefore has more time to strengthen family relationships. Planning also reduces the potential for conflicts in the business and between family members by providing a structure to deal explicitly with important family questions, which all too often remain implicit. The planning process enables the family to address these hidden issues especially around inherently difficult topics such as capital (money), careers (work), and control (decision making). It also serves to strengthen boundaries between the family and the business by offering a forum to discuss family concerns or issues that might not otherwise be properly discussed – or even worse, become part of the business' agenda.

Just like business planning, where a critical activity is developing human talent, family planning must address the development of the family's skills and capabilities for leadership and ownership, especially in the next generation. Founders and their children generally do not discuss ownership roles and responsibilities, but as the family grows they need to clarify them. What are the rights and responsibilities of the family owners? And how do family members communicate their concerns about the business' performance? When the family agrees on guidelines it creates more time for constructive efforts and less conflict on specific issues or decisions. Generally families will require a longer period of time to develop planning processes compared with their businesses. Families, especially after the Sibling Partnership phase, need to build working relationships and trust, and to begin by exploring highly emotional issues such as family values, vision, and commitment.

Throughout this book we will meet families that engage in parallel planning, each one in their own unique style. A few do it across all areas of the business; others use it in specific parts of the business, to deal with very specific questions and issues. Some do it in a more ad hoc manner; others do it more systematically. But all have experienced clear benefits through planning and managing the business and the family in a parallel process that recognizes their interdependency. We will use real examples from many leading family businesses around the world to demonstrate how the *Parallel Planning Process* can be used to create value for the family enterprise.

THE *PARALLEL PLANNING PROCESS*

Many business families espouse values and a vision that suggest a strong commitment to their firm's future success but fail to take the action for planning, investment and governance required to support the business' long-term performance. The *Parallel Planning Process* is a five-step strategic tool to help business families explore their role as owners and is designed specifically to address three weaknesses often found in family businesses:

- limited family communication about family and business activities
- a lack of a professional process for decision making about the two systems
- accountability for family and business performance.

This chapter introduces the five planning steps, each of which will be further discussed in later chapters. It will be clear from the discussion of the five steps that they are interrelated, and that business and family actions are often difficult to distinguish from one another.

Effective business families, who are concerned about their performance, work hard to integrate their values and vision with strategy, investment, and governance activities. The new *Parallel Planning Process* meets this challenge with five interrelated and interdependent action steps for the family and business: values, vision, planning, investment, and governance (see Figure 2.1).

Figure 2.1 *The family and business planning action steps*

Business Actions

There is logic to starting any planning process with an exploration of values but unfortunately this is not the way family businesses operate. In normal circumstances, if a family is struggling with conflicts over say the dividend rate, its members will often want to discuss the issue immediately rather than taking a big-picture view. Business families are action-driven and often see exploring values as a luxury reserved for large, publicly owned corporations. But because the five planning steps are interrelated, the family's thinking and action on dividends must be analyzed as a part of their values, vision, planning, and investment to create alignment.

Step 1: Family values and business culture

Business families of all cultures, from the Cargill-MacMillans of the American Midwest (whom we met in earlier in this chapter) to the Tangs of the Far East (whom we met in Chapter 1), are driven by values that reflect their shared beliefs, experiences, and goals. The first step of the *Parallel Planning Process* is to clarify family values in order to begin the process of developing the family's shared vision. When an entrepreneur creates a business there is a personal commitment to the business' success that aligns values and actions. It is important to recognize that a family's values are the most important influence on vision, strategy, investment, and governance.

Figure 2.2 *Family values and business culture*

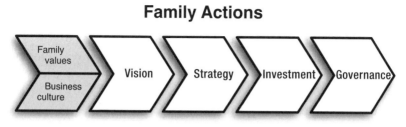

Family values

The first step is to clarify family values so that they can be written down and shared to explore the family's interests based on family beliefs, legacies, common experiences, and individual concerns. It may sound obvious that a family needs to be actively interested in any business it owns, but this is not always the case, as we discussed in the Bancroft story in Chapter 1. Sometimes the changes in family commitment over time can be disruptive or even harmful. It is during these generational transitions that the family needs to explore family commitment, and specifically how the family's vision is supported by investment of their human and financial capital.

The family's values are the starting point for the *Parallel Planning Process* and creating a platform for decisions about the business vision, strategy, investment, and governance. The family's values focus on a shared picture of how the family contributes to supporting the business' future success. Pernod Ricard, the world's second largest wine and spirits group, recently completed a major acquisition with its purchase of the Absolut brand. The family's entrepreneurial values support a vision of global market leadership. The acquisition of a global brand was a reflection of family values about growth and entrepreneurial behavior that has been driving the company since its founding as a small pastis distiller in the South of France. The family and business values, vision, strategy, investment, and governance are aligned because the family values and vision supported this major acquisition.[4]

Family values can also reflect how the family interacts with employees and other stakeholders. Timpson, the fast-growing British shoe-repair and key-cutting company, which now offers many other services, demonstrates a caring, family-like relationship with the company's staff. Employees get a day off on their birthday, the company provides time at holiday homes for employees, and operates a fund for people in financial distress. It is also active in the community, including a recent initiative to hire ex-offenders and set up a training centre in a Liverpool jail.

For John Timpson, the firm's chairman, this support and respect for employees and work in the community is nothing to do with corporate social responsibility; rather, it is an expression of family values. "We don't see this as a responsibility. It's not about giving something back;

we do it because we enjoy doing it, because it matters to us," he says. "We are able to do it because we have the privilege of owning a profitable business. Other business owners might have an interest in a football team or they might buy paintings; we happen to do other things that we care about."

Business families need to develop a shared understanding about the family's values, which ultimately shape the family's vision and decision making, and the culture of the business. Values act as powerful glue for the business and family, and are also a powerful rudder in times of change and upheaval. Clarifying and agreeing on values is a key step toward reducing potential conflicts and encouraging entrepreneurial strategies. Although the family may not fully agree on all of the values, and conflicts may arise about the family's participation in the planning process, this is a positive and crucial step toward helping the family assess its current situation and begin to make plans that resolve the issues.

"Our values are the cornerstone of what really holds us together today," says Grant E. Gordon of William Grant & Sons, Ltd, a fifth-generation family-owned business and one of the largest Scotch whisky makers in the world, "We are proud we are an independent family company. We are proud of our heritage as a Scottish family company and conscious of the privilege we have of being a family, and naturally take pride in our products and their quality."

Family business culture

Business families have values and their businesses have an organizational culture. The firm's culture is a shared set of beliefs held by the organization and its stakeholders about how and why the firm is successful. The culture can be a powerful tool for motivating employees and creating behavioral norms that support the firm's strategy. The firm's culture is strongly influenced by the family's values and behaviors as owners and leaders. Pictet & Cie, the Swiss private bank, uses its marketing to communicate the owners' three core values of respect, integrity, and independence. Like most family businesses, Pictet's actions are driven by these values and their work environment is based on them. In times of stress and uncertainty these values are fundamental in demonstrating to employees and other stakeholders what behaviors support the bank's continued success.

Business culture is an important topic in management literature, so we are not going to include a long discussion, except to point out that family business culture can be an advantage over more anonymously owned and widely traded firms, where financial performance dominates all aspects of culture, strategy, and rewards. These firms may lack a strong culture that creates a sense of belonging or human connection. They are driven by extensive control and management information systems using policies and procedures, performance reviews, audits and budgets, and a hierarchy of approvals rather than trust or belief in a shared purpose. In contrast a family business culture, built on human relationships and demonstrated concern for all stakeholders, encourages long-term thinking and stewardship. A family that shares its stories and history with its employees as a tool for encouraging creativity and entrepreneurship can build an empowered firm.

Step 2: Family and business vision

The family's shared vision for the business and for itself is the main criterion for making decisions and the second action step in the *Parallel Planning Process*. Discussion about the shared vision is critical for helping the family articulate their thinking and develop a consensus about the family and business strategies to pursue. Family members who see the business primarily as a source of dividends and wealth will not have the same vision as those who interesting in reinvesting the profits in a high-growth strategy to strengthen the business' competitive position.

Figure 2.3 *Family and business vision*

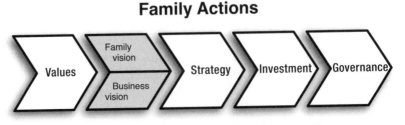

Business vision

A family business vision consists of two interrelated parts. The first is the state of the business in a given future time frame, say ten years. What does the family want the business to become in terms of impact, size, reputation, markets, financial structure, number of employees, and profits? This is a very quantifiable discussion that, when it results in clear agreement, establishes the parameters for the second part of the vision: a clear understanding of how the family contributes to and benefits from the business' success. The *Parallel Planning Process* allows families to explore first their vision for the business, then how family ownership becomes a competitive advantage to the business.

Family vision

The exploration of family vision also has a transformational effect, reframing family conversation from "what's in it for me?" to "how do we contribute?" The idea of the family's contribution to the business' continued success is the basis for stewardship – leaving the next generation and other stakeholders a more valuable asset than you inherited. The family's long-term vision can become a competitive advantage to the business. Developing a shared vision influences family behavior by encouraging a long-term perspective on plans and decisions.

Many families make their vision the guide to investment and strategic actions. For example, Roche, the giant Swiss pharmaceutical company, focused its efforts on diseases that are difficult to treat because the Hoffmann family's controlling ownership gave them the benefit of a very long-term investment horizon. As André Hoffmann, non-executive vice president of Roche Holding Ltd, says,

> The goal of our family owners is based on a duty to pass on a stronger business to the next generation. This creates incredible glue that focuses on the best interest of the family. We also have a sense of responsibility to our "compagnons de la route."[5]

Step 3: Family and business strategy

Strategic planning for a family firm is the same as in any other firm – except for the ownership and family concerns discussed throughout this book. Strategic planning is the tool to ensure ongoing communication that helps management, board, and family align the family's expectations with the business' needs.

Participation planning for the family is very different. Businesses focus on technical tasks (marketing, finance, distribution), whereas families are about social tasks and human relationships. The goal of planning for the family is to prepare its members for participation in the business as executives, owners, and board members, and in new family enterprise activities such as a family council, family office, or family foundation. This often means helping individual members develop new skills and knowledge, to create more effective interpersonal relationships, and to ensure that there is sufficient leadership and governance talent to fill roles in both the family and the business.

Figure 2.4   *Family and business strategy*

Family Actions

Business Actions

Business strategy

Strategic business planning provides a systematic way to ask critical business questions. What market opportunities should we exploit? What resources do we need to develop to compete successfully in the future? What is the required level of financial investment? These questions challenge historical business practices and allow the exploration of new opportunities and actions. It is at this point that the family's investment decisions shape the actual strategy, as the owners determine, often with the board, the balance between reinvestment and dividends.

Designing a business strategy aligned with the family's vision will ensure that everyone shares a clear picture of the company's future and of the resources available to support the strategy. In a family business, management needs to consider the family's values and vision carefully to ensure that the owners are agreed on their intentions and commitment. The interaction of the family's vision and commitment drives the planning process for family investment decisions. For example, if a family decides to reduce its investments in capital expenditures by increasing dividends, it would be very difficult for management to develop an aggressive growth strategy using only internally generated funding. Measuring the family's commitment, based on the investment of its human and financial capital, is a critical concern for management in planning the firm's long-term strategies and investments.

Participation strategy

Family discussions about values and vision are the starting point for exploring the kind of participation that sustains multi-generational ownership. It is also participation strategy that presents the biggest challenges of the *Parallel Planning Process* because of emotions, differences in talent and motivation, and family relationships. Business interactions are professional and temporal, meaning that plans require clarity and a relatively short time frame; family relationships, in contrast, are emotional and last for life. Family issues, like succession, careers, and ownership, are highly personal – making it simpler to avoid rather than confront them. Yet as the number of generations grows and the business becomes more complex, the family has to become more professional in its interactions – clarifying decision making, planning, and leadership roles for its members.

One important reason for undertaking family and business strategic planning in parallel is to ensure that the two systems' goals, plans, and policies are coordinated to focus efforts and prevent conflicts. A family business in which family and management are strongly aligned around the future is positioned to develop a clearer strategic direction and mutually supportive goals.

Step 4: Investing human and financial capital

Often we discover that the lack of family investment in human and financial capital (leadership and money) is the stumbling block to business growth and continuing the family's ownership legacy. The lack of financial investment results in lost business opportunities, and a lack of investment of human capital results in family conflicts, uncertain leadership, lack of decisions, and no accountability.

Investment decisions are always difficult because they have an impact on so many family concerns: lifestyles, reputations, wealth creation and protection, business growth and sustainability, and the family's psychological connection to the business. A business family that wants to explore its future together needs to answer two questions. First, what is the potential of the family business for long-term value creation? Second, what level of financial investment (reinvestment versus dividends) and human capital (family leadership and governance talent) is required to support the business' future success?

Figure 2.5   *Investing human and financial capital*

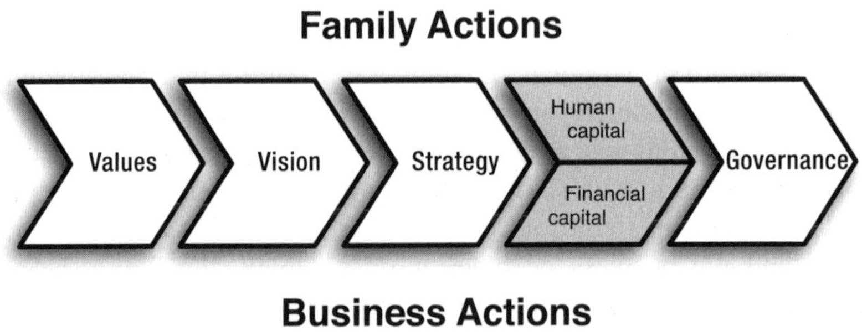

Family Actions

Business Actions

Financial capital investment

A business family needs to think strategically about its investment to ensure that the business is fully utilizing the family's commitment to exploit market opportunities. The Ülker family business, Turkey's leader in chocolates and biscuits manufacturing, is a good example of how family commitment should be expressed. When Godiva, one of the world's top chocolate brands, was offered for sale, the family was prepared to outbid many larger global players because it knew the strategic value to its firm. The family owners were fully supportive of the Godiva acquisition and enabled the business' management to outmaneuver many significantly larger competitors. The Ülkers are an entrepreneurial family with a small group of owners, but a larger family needs the discipline of a planning process to ensure that the family and business remain aligned.

Human capital investment

A committed business family also needs to consider investment of the family's human capital. This second form of investment, especially in capable leaders and owners, represents the family members' willingness and capability to support the family business. Rolf Abdon, founder and CEO of Abdon Mills, with facilities in Europe and North America and operations in Asia, shares how important the development of family human capital was in his "family" business success:

> I feel like mine is a second or third generation family business because my father was the CEO of the largest grain miller in Northern Europe. He was a non-family executive and I inherited from him not a business but something more important: his knowledge, attitudes, wisdom and experience. In many ways it was better to inherit these soft skills rather than a business.

A family's investment of its human and financial capital clearly demonstrates a belief that its ownership creates a competitive advantage for the business. Baron Jean-Pierre Berghmans, chairman of the Executive Board at the Lhoist Group in Belgium, speaking to a group of INSEAD MBAs, argued that "You must have the full commitment of the shareholders in a family business if you want to succeed." He cites his family's commitment to investing capital and to serving as executives or directors as two factors that have helped sustain the company's spectacular growth. When family owners are active, they are more likely to keep a sharp eye on performance – their own and their competitors' – and avoid falling into the trap of complacency.

Step 5: Family and business governance

Governance is the final action step in the *Parallel Planning Process*, essential to ensuring that families and management work together on decision making and accountability. Three key governance mechanisms are common in family businesses: the board of directors, family meetings or family council, and family agreements. The board of directors represents the business, employees, and shareholders for addressing critical decisions, protecting business viability, and ensuring management performance. Family meetings serve a similar function, but address only family issues, such as communication, relationships, education, agreements, conflict, social activities, and philanthropy. Family agreements are written policies (also known as family constitutions, charters, or protocols), which address all the topics connecting the family and business discussed in this book (such as, family values, employment policies, dividend policy, and roles and responsibilities of ownership).

Figure 2.6   *Business and family governance*

Family Actions

Business Actions

Business governance

All businesses have some form of board of directors, whether it exists for legal purposes only or as a critical tool for strategic planning, business direction, and management accountability. An often-missed opportunity is the board's potential contribution to the strategic planning process through identifying critical issues, discussing possible scenarios, and challenging management's thinking. The board can also develop policies to guide business activities, investment, and compensation, and to monitor management's performance. The importance of the board's role increases over time, as the business and family grow and become more complex.

Family governance

Thinking about family governance is often foreign to many business families. "We're a family; we do not need a board!" is a popular reaction. Yet expanding business families require formal planning, decision-making, and problem-solving processes just like their businesses. Families need to make decisions about employment, board representation, dividends, and investment. In the start-up stage the founder handles these issues, as a part of operating the business. When the family moves to the second generation of siblings or beyond, or if there is a separation of management and ownership roles, a new structure is needed to make decisions.

Grant E. Gordon, speaking at a Kellogg School of Management Conference, shared a powerful thought:

> Even though the company is run by an outside management team and chaperoned by a professional board it is important that the family has oversight and that we discuss the key strategic issues. You have a governing structure with, on one hand, the family council, which represents the shareholder group in family issues, the vision, and the various other issues under our family charter. And you have the supervisory board, which really sits on top of the business to make sure it's successful.

Who is flying the family airplane?

One metaphor we learned from colleague Ivan Lansberg that may help business families, especially those headed by founders and entrepreneurs, to think about the need for family and business parallel planning is to ask how the family would deal with owning an airplane together. Everyone agrees that flying a plane is a serious undertaking that requires planning and decision making. Owning a family business is a lot like owning an airplane because it requires careful planning about the final destination (vision), crew (family and non- family executives), and flight plan (business strategy) before attempting to fly. This parallel planning is fundamental as it reduces the chances of having too many pilots in the cockpit trying to fly the plane to many different destinations.

If the family and management have a clear vision, they will know how much fuel they will need, how many pilots they require, how many passengers they can carry, and the type of flight plan they need to prepare. If the pilots develop a flight plan (business strategy) based on where the passengers (owners) want to go, considering the weather conditions (economic environment) and the air traffic controllers' instructions (board of directors), then there will be a shared commitment to everyone staying on the plane.

There is little doubt about who should fly the plane – a professional pilot with sufficient flight hours, full certification, and an agreed flight plan. Staying the course also requires instruments (financial reports) and air traffic control (governance), as it is these systems that ensure not only that the plane is flying to the right destination, but also that proper maintenance (investment) is completed to keep the it airworthy.

One question is seldom asked on planes but frequently leads to family business conflict: Who can change the flight plans in mid-air? Many family firms struggle with the answer – is it the board, management team, or the family? After all, each of these groups has a deep commitment to the business and often long experience. We would suggest that there is no single right answer. This is a fundamental governance issue that must be clarified in family agreements and governance processes so that none of the passengers ends up trying to pilot the plane – unless of course they have the requisite license and flying hours.

A *PARALLEL PLANNING PROCESS* USER GUIDE

As readers may have noticed, this is a different kind of family business book. It does not aim to provide solutions to all the specific problems or issues that arise in family business – so do not look up "succession" in the index and expect to find nine steps to managing family business succession. What this book does provide is a systematic planning process that enables members of a business family to work together and deal with the key issues that will allow them to become more effective and committed owners of their family firm – to create a competitive advantage for the business.

The *Parallel Planning Process* allows families to explore their commitment, values, and vision, to agree on roles, to develop processes, and to ensure timely decision making and accountability through governance. It is a powerful and proven system but does not have to be implemented from A to Z. Our work with the *Parallel Planning Process* suggests a few principles that are effective for business families. These insights are offered to encourage families to start the process and not to be discouraged by setbacks.

■ *It is not a plan or an agreement unless it is written down.* The world is full of ideas, most of which are never acted on. Families need to write notes and minutes as a basis for developing agreement and action planning. These notes do not need to be a final complete document. But they are a beginning. And there is a paper trail. The family's first written document is a simple code of conduct drafted at the start of the first meeting (see Chapter 3). Minutes from all meetings are essential to clarifying information and ensuring that everyone is included in the process, even if they can't attend a meeting.

■ *The entire family does not need to take part in the family planning process.* Planning works best when interested and committed parties are involved as a task force that represents the entire family. Start the process with everyone who expresses an interest (if the group is large you may need to create smaller task forces to work on different parts of the process), and hopefully others will join you, when they feel able. If an important family member refuses to participate, begin the process without them, but make sure that they – and the entire family – know about all discussions and plans. There are no secrets.

■ *The only place to begin a process of change is with yourself.* At the end of the day, only you can change your behavior (unless it is against your will, which does not count). When you change your behavior you will influence changes in the way others react to you, but your goal is to change yourself first and foremost. New behaviors are necessary to create new solutions.

■ *Get professional help.* If the family gets stuck and cannot communicate or organize effectively it may be necessary to ask a trusted family advisor, board member, family business consultant, or professional mediator to join the process and get things moving. If you repeat the same ineffective behaviors you can be reasonably certain of having the same outcomes over and over again. Often families get stuck because they have not learned to work together or they do not fully understand the issues created by family business ownership. So another possible action is to attend a family business executive program like those offered at INSEAD and the Kellogg School of Management.

■ *Some aspects of the family planning process will be ongoing without a final plan or full agreement.* This is fine. Families need time, and sometimes agreeing to start a project is a good first step. Families need to work with what is possible, rather than try and achieve too much – even small changes in the system can lead to larger changes elsewhere. Some families do not complete all of the *Parallel Planning Process* steps. This is not a problem if the family is able to work effectively together to develop plans and actions.

■ *Take small steps and follow the path of least resistance.* At any moment there will be several possible priorities competing for the family's attention. Some of these will be bigger and more challenging; others will be smaller and more manageable. Sometimes it is better to focus on the low-hanging fruit, to make progress with a smaller issue than take on a more challenging one. This makes people more confident as they learn to work together and gain confidence in their own ability to solve problems. In addition, the impetus and momentum can be applied to other business challenges. The decision on how to proceed is always with your task force or family.

■ *Proactive family planning is a learned behavior.* In our experience families change when they need to. There is usually a trigger for the desire to deal with a particular problem. Again the principle here is a simple one – learning to plan and take action is better than waiting for a problem or conflict to arise. If the family's concerns for planning or decision making are driven by conflict over an issue, it is important to get professional help to reduce the pain. If someone's son or daughter was refused employment in the family business because of an unwritten agreement, then the family should address the issue as soon a possible. Once the planning process begins, many families maintain an annual agenda of priorities and work through the topics at regularly scheduled meetings. It is important to be proactive so that discussions and decisions are not based on a specific family member or incident.

■ *There is no single path for business families to follow in order to address their planning needs.* It may take several years for the family and business plans to interconnect fully and for the goals of each to become fully aligned. The example of Cargill demonstrates this point: its planning process is ongoing, developed over many years, and based on continuous improvement. Parallel planning for the future alignment of the business and for the future of the family is nearly always a continuous process at the heart of a successful family business.

■ *Education and training is a priority.* Again, Cargill shows the way. Planning is not possible without a knowledge and shared under-standing. And understanding has to be developed and nurtured by the family as a part of the family's participation plan discussed in Chapter 5. In the end, the equation is simple: Education enhances the family's development of human capital as a competitive advantage.

Part II

Creating Human Meaning

3   Family Values and Business Culture

Family Actions

Business Actions

The importance of family business values was clearly demonstrated by Whitney MacMillan, the last family CEO of Cargill, when he stated, "As a company, we have believed in the same values for 125 years, even though we have changed the business every five years." It is natural to explore family values at the start of the *Parallel Planning Process* because planning represents how the family perceives itself, what is important, and how it behaves. Family businesses, like all for-profit organizations, are driven by values related to competition, wealth, responsibility, fairness, and hard work. Counterbalancing these economic priorities are family values about love, cohesion, self-esteem, and caring.

When family values are extended into the business, they provide a powerful source of strength and continuity to mediate financial priorities and shape more humanistic plans and actions. Values can act as a powerful rudder in times of change or upheaval, and can act as a kind of glue for business and family success. Crucially, family values are a source of competitive advantage to many successful family businesses.

A family business' beliefs and values start with the founder, reflecting his or her behaviors as the family leader and entrepreneur.[1] Over time, these values are shared by a wider group of family members – passed from one generation to the next and renewed each time. Although family values are not always explicit they have a big impact on company culture and the way a business operates. Without shared values, family business success is unlikely because disagreements over priorities and decisions become a source of struggle and conflict. The first step of the *Parallel Planning Process* is thus for family members to explore, agree, and write down the values critical to themselves and their business.

Family values are in many ways the family's attempt to express who they are, to make meaning for themselves – and a guiding star for the business. Values are unique to each family, representing a narrative about how their behaviors make them successful. Success is always socially constructed, which means that it is expressed or interpreted in the context of each family's experience and relationships. One family may interpret success by financial performance, where another measures it in terms of family reputation or service to others. Values also form the basis of performance standards or expectation within the family. Again, one family may see higher education as an important measure of accomplishment while another would see work experience as the real indicator of achievement.

The family's values set the internal standards of behavior so that members will know what to expect from each other. There is a classic line that many parents repeat when a child acts inappropriately: "That is not how we behave in this family." When families act in accordance with shared values, trust develops. Shared assumptions, norms, beliefs, and experiences also help family members understand each other's motivations. Common values can frame decisions and planning by encouraging cooperation, promoting relationships, reducing harmful conflict, and enabling effective responses to crises.

Family values can serve many different purposes in business families. In some families they express a code of family conduct; in others they reinforce the organization's culture or underpin the firm's business strategy. In some families they frame social responsibility, while in others they support philanthropy or spell out next-generation leadership behaviors. Values also act as the glue for building and sustaining long-term family and interpersonal relationships across generations and branches. Agreed values are important to the next generation in supporting how they will work together. Family values shape thinking about issues such as careers and compensation. For example, if a family value is equality then paying based on seniority or time on the job makes sense. If the core value is high performance then bonuses may be more appropriate.

Shared values are the bedrock of stability but they can also be a roadblock to change, especially during generational transitions. Business families struggle as generations and branches multiply, because the same values are interpreted differently according to experiences, education, and changes in the business world. Members of the senior generation, who accepted equal salaries, may have sent their children to top business schools, where they were taught that compensation is based on qualification and contribution.

This chapter explores the first parallel planning step of discussing and confirming family values. This activity shapes the ground rules, goals, and possible actions for the entire planning process. Discussing values also creates an opportunity for exploring differences in a constructive and general manner rather than experiencing conflicts over specific issues. The planning process allows business families to share, transmit, and negotiate family values that may need updating to reflect current practices and beliefs. The most serious family conflicts arise not from disagreements about business actions, but from a violation of family values.

FAMILY VALUES AND BUSINESS PERFORMANCE

At a recent Kellogg School of Management family business conference, participants were asked what they felt was the biggest advantage of a family firm. A strong values-based culture was rated as one of the most important. Strong values matter. Family values have an impact on the way family businesses operate, the business' culture and strategy, and performance expectations – whether explicitly stated or not. Consider the way in which Sam Walton's thrift affected all aspects of Walmart, the US retail chain, and its famously successful strategy. How many multi-billion-dollar global companies ask their senior executives to fly coach and share hotel rooms? How many get employees to bring pencils from home to save costs? The importance of this business mythology lies not in the direct savings created by the specific actions. Rather it reflects a way of seeing the business and how "we" compete. This expense-sensitive culture underlies the entire Walmart strategy of being able to sell products at competitive prices because it has the industry's lowest cost structure.

A family's core values concerning how employees and customers are treated, for example, or how the family defines its responsibilities to stakeholders, inevitably influence the development of business plans, policies, and family agreements, whether implicit or discussed as part of the *Parallel Planning Process*. The Cargill and MacMillan families discussed in Chapter 2 clearly believe in the value of long-term investment, paying low dividends, and plowing back profits into the business. This has had a large impact on the company's strategy by enabling investment in projects that publicly traded peers could not justify because of quarterly and annual performance benchmarks.

Many long-lived family companies use core values as a basis for defining their family's relationships to the business' mission. Take the Eu family of Singapore. When their great-grandfather set up his one-man shop dispensing traditional Chinese medicines and herbs, it became Eu Yan Sang – a combination of his family name and the phrase "Yan Sang," which means "caring for mankind." But if the family does not share a set of beliefs about what the business means to the family and what the family's responsibilities are to the business, there can be unproductive conflict – as was the case in Eu Yan Sang during the 1980s. An ongoing series of family conflicts over trade names, strategy, and control almost destroyed the business.[2]

FAMILY VALUES IN PRACTICE

This section explores how family values can focus on different aspects of the family business system. It is important to note that each of these examples addresses a different aspect of the family and the business – but because family businesses are a system, the values for family members, the business strategy or social responsibility have an impact on all aspects of planning for both family and business. A business family do not need multiple sets of values for all their different concerns. One clear set of values addressing family priorities creates a shared ethos that supports planning and decision making.

Family values and stewardship

Family stewardship is a value stipulating that each generation will pass on a family business that is healthier and more valuable to future generations. Stewards recognize that they are making decisions for their children's children, and therefore consider the long-term interests not only of the current owners but also of future owners – and often of other stakeholders in the firm. Families can encourage stewardship by reviewing important actions based on future outcomes and consequences.

Stewardship is a core value at Warburtons, the leading British family-owned baker. Jonathan Warburton, chairman of the company, says:

> I see my role as being a steward, to leave the business in a stronger position that than when I came to work here for the first time. … That's a big part of why I get up in the morning: a restlessness to be better, to improve the business, to leave a legacy for the family. There is no doubt that it's very important that my immediate family feel proud of what we have and what we have achieved.

Craigie Zildjian, member of the well-known cymbal-making Armenian-American family, has similar views on stewardship as the key to longevity: "A good part of [our] identity comes from [the] 383-year-old tradition of making the finest cymbals in the world," she said on *BusinessWeek* website Business Exchange. "As such, we consider ourselves stewards to the business, ensuring that the business gets whatever it needs."

Taking a stewardship approach brings a profound change in perspective that demands sound planning, timely decision making, and rigorous accountability for both the family and business systems. The reality is that stewardship values require much work but offer great rewards. Business families will have to trade short-term profits for sustained performance. Another important part of stewardship thinking is to

Figure 3.1 *Murugappa family values and stewardship*

Bill of Responsibilities: Individuals to the Company

Adhere to ethical norms in all dealings with shareholders, employees, customers, financial institutions, and government.

Provide value for money to customers through quality products and services.

Treat our people with respect and concern; provide opportunities to learn, contribute and advance; recognize and reward initiative, innovativeness, and creativity.

Maintain an organizational climate conducive to trust, open communication, and team spirit.

Maintain a style of operations befitting our size, but reflecting moderation and humility.

Manage environment effectively for harnessing opportunities.

Discharge responsibilities to various sections of society and preserve environment.

Grow in an accelerated manner, consistent with values and beliefs, by continuous organization renewal.

clarify the family's responsibilities to the business and to itself, as India's Murugappa Group demonstrates.

Murugappa Group is a fifth-generation family business and one of India's largest business organizations, with sales of US$1 billion and over 23,000 employees.[3] During the last ten years the family has restructured its ownership and management, building a competitive advantage based on values about individual members' responsibilities to the business and how they work together (see Figure 3.1). In a recent interview an outside board member described Murugappa's success as follows: "If you ask the man in the street what he thinks of the Murugappa Group, he will say they are impeccable in terms of their values, but very conservative, very slow."

The family's values combine religious beliefs and business practices in a unique blend of spiritualism and economics. The values that guided the early generations of the family became the guiding principles for a new ownership and leadership model focused on the future. The former chairman, M. V. Subbiah, shared his nephew's explanation of the family's role:

We consider ourselves custodians to a heritage and trustees to a tradition, both built on togetherness, trust, mutual respect, ethical values and, above all, dignity, independence, and discipline. As the scope and magnitude of the family and business leadership changes, we are preparing ourselves for the great challenges ahead.

In 1996, on being named chairman, Mr. Subbiah, working with the senior family leader and a trusted and respected family advisor, began the process of leading a family team in discussions about business leadership and governance. The goal was to balance a need for strong management in the group's five operating companies with the family's values, strategic thinking, and governance. The working group met for almost two years to discuss how the family could create a new model of ownership and governance in which they would become governor-owners rather owner-managers. The outcome was a renewed commitment to the values of individual responsibility and stewardship, to be achieved by aligning the five companies more closely, becoming more objective, developing the talents of the non-family managing directors, and continuing to strengthen the governance processes.

Family values and the organization's culture

The founder shapes the firm's culture directly through his or her leadership, and indirectly through the children who succeed him or her as owners or leaders of the business. Nowhere is this truer than at SC Johnson, the global household cleaning manufacturer. At the age of 53, Samuel Curtis Johnson launched first a flooring company and then diversified into floor wax when he noticed his customers needed a product to preserve their new floors.[4] As the reputation of Johnson's Prepared Wax spread, he redirected his efforts, and soon became first a regional, then a national, and finally an international leader for wax products. His entrepreneurial values shaped the development of the Johnson Wax culture, which embraced innovation and pushed the envelope in its product development, international expansion, marketing, and employee relationships (see Figure 3.2). During the years preceding his death, at age 86, he continued to grow and strengthen the business, running national magazine advertising and offering his employees an expanded set of benefits including paid vacations and profit sharing.

After the founder's death, his son Herbert assumed the presidency. Herbert had joined his father at age 18 when the family business was

Figure 3.2 *Family values and organization culture*

Johnson Family Values

Entrepreneurship

Innovation

Risk Taking

Knowledge and technology

Employee welfare

Customer Relationship Marketing

Vision

Proactivity

Global thinking

just two years old, so he was a part of the founding entrepreneurial team. He continued in the family tradition of innovation by building the company's first research and development laboratory (which produced dozens of new cleaning products), expanding into Canada, offering additional employee benefits (such as a 40-hour working week), and creating the Racine Community Chest. This charitable fund was designed to meet social needs of Racine (Wisconsin), where the firm was headquartered. Just before his death in 1928 Herbert articulated the family's core belief that, "the goodwill of people (employees and customers) is the only enduring thing in any business. It is the sole substance ... the rest is shadow."

The unexpected death of his father at age 60 thrust Herbert Jr. into the role of president and chief operating officer. Herbert Jr., also known as H. F., led the company through the ten years of the Great Depression, and despite a 40 percent drop in sales, stayed loyal to the family values and did not lay off one employee. Once the company was stabilized he continued the family's entrepreneurial style of management. He opened new subsidiaries in France and South America, introduced more that two dozen new products, created pension and hospitalization plans for employees, and expanded the family's philanthropic efforts. In the United States, Johnson Wax became one of the first national advertisers in the new medium of radio. Working to build an even more innovative company, H. F. hired

Frank Lloyd Wright, a leading modern architect, to design a corporate headquarters with a revolutionary open-plan layout, which encouraged communication and sharing across departments and functions.

H. F.'s son, Sam, unexpectedly took over the firm when his father suffered a serious stroke. Sam's first major assignment at Johnson Wax was to develop and head the New Products Department. Under his leadership the firm developed four major new products: Raid insecticide, OFF insect repellant, Pledge furniture polish, and Glade air freshener. By 1960 these four new products accounted for 35 percent of the company's sales. During Sam's tenure the company expanded to 45 countries and sales of over US$5 billion. All of these family members share a value of entrepreneurial behavior as a basis for their management and leadership.

Family values and a code of conduct

Family values have also been essential to the success of the Huizenga family, according to P. J. Huizenga, son of the family business' founder Wayne Huizenga. Speaking at a Kellogg School of Management family business conference, he shared nine core Huizenga family values that formed a strong code of conduct for the family (see Figure 3.3). Sibling

Figure 3.3 *Family values and family conduct*

Huizenga Family Values

Work hard

Honor and have faith in God

Establish strong relationships

Do things differently

Take risks

Be a servant leader

Treat others with respect

Give back to others

Be humble

partnership can be difficult, so having a clear code of conduct helps reduce misunderstanding and smoothes decision making. P. J. Huizenga said:

> My father and uncles used these values ... transforming what was once Huizenga & Sons Private Scavenger into Waste Management, servicing over 27 million residents around the globe. These values were passed to each generation through my great-grandfather's example and through family get-togethers. Passing down family values from generation to generation has helped to make a highly successful business culture for us. I don't think we would have attained the level of success we have without these core values.

As the younger Huizenga suggests, it is passing on and updating family values across generations that creates the challenges for business families. A father shares his values directly through every action and word; it is a direct communication to his children by a powerful family figure. The father's status and credibility create a strong emotional impact on his children about how a business family should act and what makes you successful in business. This impact is lost with each succeeding generation, and after the second generation, it is unlikely that any of the family will have worked directly with the founder for any significant period of time. This means that the family needs to institutionalize its family values and develop processes to transmit them across generations.

Family values and business strategy

The family's values add synergy based on a unity of purpose between the family and the business' strategy. This is particularly evident at Italy's Beretta, a world leader in weapons manufacturing and one of the world's oldest family-owned and operated businesses.[5] At Beretta there is a direct connection between the family and the business in every plan, decision, and action. Unlike most 500-year-old family businesses Beretta has no separation of ownership and management roles. The family leads all aspects of the business. It is clear from their family values that this is a business family with a heavy emphasis on the business (see Figure 3.4).

Figure 3.4 *Family values for business strategy*

Beretta Family Values

"Prudence and Audacity"

Personal freedom: The "Power of One"

Invest in new technology every year

Quality without compromise

Ancient art of craftsmanship with the latest technology

A finely tuned organization is crucial to success

Believe in and like the product you make

Systematic innovation: processes, procedures, and equipment

The family's clear values have also helped make ownership and management succession transitions a time for the next generation to identify new opportunities and strategies. The long tenure of family leadership creates stability and a sound base for the next generation to learn the business and prepare their thinking for the next tenure. Beretta's strong family values enable successors to question long-held business paradigms, drive new technologies, and pursue new ventures more aggressively. In family business, the key to renewing strategy is often the effective transmission of values to succeeding generations. When this is accomplished, family companies maintain a powerful ability to innovate and sustain their entrepreneurial cultures.

Family values and next-generation leadership

Developing capable leaders and owners is one of the most challenging tasks for any organization. It is even more difficult for family enterprises in Asia and the Middle East because they often face additional complexities from conflicting business and family values and different generational expectations. Environmental forces, including changing social values, new technology, increased competition, political threats,

Figure 3.5 *Family values for next-generation leadership*

Al Jaber Family Values

Take responsibility

Listen and learn

Treat people fairly

Maintain our family heritage

Pure hearts and moral values

Be generous

Empower people to solve problems

Leadership of people and how to motivate

and physical constraints also place demands on the family firm and its future leaders. This means that the next generation of family members face obstacles to becoming capable leaders and owners.

Obaid Al Jaber, the founder and patriarch of the Emirati Jaber Group, is clear that next-generation leadership success is a matter of values (see Figure 3.5).[6] First, like all executives, family members need to perform at a high level – his son and daughter must demonstrate leadership and perform as well as any non-family employee to avoid eroding respect for family management. Second, they must earn the trust of their stakeholders and mostly importantly their employees, who are often amongst their toughest critics. Third, the next generation must manage the family heritage so that other stakeholders do not view the change in leadership as a challenge to the family's relationships.

If they are honest, most senior generation family business leaders will tell you that their greatest fear is that their children will not be prepared for the leadership responsibilities that a successful family enterprise imposes. One problem is that the senior leaders themselves are not always clear what criteria make for successful next generation leaders. At the Al Jaber Group this was not an issue because the founder realized early on that, while managerial skills are important, his two children's success as the top executives in his company was based on their values and leadership. Obaid Al Jaber insisted that he would not focus on financial and technical performance when choosing a successor but rather on the individual's ability to interact ethically and wisely with a diverse group of employees. He believed that the most important quality in a leader was what he called "a clean heart" – if one's heart is not pure, this will be reflected in the poor quality of one's work.

Family values and corporate social responsibility

Corporate social responsibility is seldom a key competitive advantage. But at MAS in Sri Lanka, Mahesh, Ajay, and Sharad Amalean, the three brothers who founded the clothing manufacturing firm, knew that competing against low-cost producers in other emerging economies was not a sustainable business model.[7] Uncertainties over tariffs and regulation, an ongoing civil war in Sri Lanka, and Western consumers' concerns over sweatshop practices became an opportunity to develop a business model that represented the interaction of family values and the realities of a difficult commercial environment. Again, it is important to reflect on how the Amalean family values about people's needs and philanthropy create a competitive advantage for their business (see Figure 3.6).

Figure 3.6 *Family values as social responsibility*

MAS Family Values

We embrace the UN Charter of International Human Rights & Global Compact Principle.

We do not accept any form of harassment or discrimination and work in a culture of equal opportunity, whilst recognizing the contribution that people with disabilities can make to society and work.

No persons under 18 are employed.

Our working week, including overtime does not exceed 60 hours.

We recognize the need to work in partnership with employees, encouraging them to learn, develop, contribute, and achieve a work–life balance

We provide where appropriate, a range of benefits including transport, meals, air-conditioned facilities, health, life and work place medical care, banking, and counselling.

Women are the majority – a driving force in our organizations – and care is given to reward and empower them both within the plant and the community, through "The MAS Women – Go Beyond Programme."

MAS was formed by three brothers who believed in quality and respect. Their company name reflects their commitment to each other. Mahesh Amalean, chairman of MAS Holding in Sri Lanka, explains, "The name of our company MAS (Mahesh, Ajay, and Sharad, the three brothers) represents our working relationship. The key to our success is organizing our roles around each brother's skills and a deep respect for each other." Another core value was quality and market leadership. Mahesh says:

> We never thought in terms of how big the business would grow; to us it was income our families and a chance to do what we wanted to do. Our overriding vision was to work with the best, so we consciously sought them out in order to become the best. Their performance helped us grow from bidding and manufacturing, to preferred manufacturing to preferred partners providing solutions to their product needs.

The key success factor for MAS as a manufacturing company with more than 35,000 employees in nine developing Asian countries was a reliable workforce. The traditional sweatshop model did not make good sense to a family concerned about the people it worked with. It sounds so simple, as Mahesh Amalean says: "If people we work with have their basic needs taken care of, they are freer to concentrate on the work at hand and bring out their best." These beliefs drive a strategy that puts factories near the workers so that they don't have to be away from their families, and provides free meals, on-site banking, and medical care as smart business investments. While meeting the employees' most basic needs is important, MAS has also created the Women Go Beyond program (over 90 percent of its employees are women) to help educate and empower their workforce.

The contribution that values make to the business' future success is clearly expressed in the support the Amaleans have received from major clients like Gap, Nike, Marks & Spencer, and Victoria's Secret. These global apparel retailers depend on their brand reputation and the image of their products, so MAS's HR policies and the Women Go Beyond program represent powerful marketing advantages. The vice president of compliance for Gap, Inc. explains: "We hope that we can begin to relay more information to our customers about how our products are made and that it may eventually get factored into buying decisions." This is a dramatic turnaround from the past, when large Western retailers worked to keep their suppliers hidden from the end consumer for fear of a negative customer reaction.

A global overview of family values

Family values can be quite hard to pin down. They are also dynamic, reflecting changes in the family and external world. Many families, after writing a values statement, review and discuss it annually as a part of their meeting process. The act of regularly discussing values becomes a tool for both clarifying and transmitting them across generations. This process makes the values a living part of the family's thinking rather than some abstract statement logged in the minutes of last year's annual meeting.

It is not always easy to understand what values mean in practice. What exactly are the implications of efficiency or equity as family values in terms of what the business can or cannot do? What are the limits? How do you know when a particular set of actions is not in line with the family's values? Also, values may be understood and interpreted differently by various family members. The key here is to try and make the values as explicit as possible. Our research also suggests several specific behaviors that tend to be reflected in family business values (see Table 3.1). Most business families will develop values statements that reflect some combination of these behaviors.

FAMILY BUSINESS RESPONSIBILITY AND FAIRNESS

How a family defines its responsibilities and deals with fairness are two higher-order values or overriding philosophies that shape the family's personal style, influence its relationships, and influence management practice. These higher values raise the two most important questions about the family's priorities and how it works together. First, whose interests should take priority: those of the business or those of the family? Second, how does the family communicate, plan and make decisions together? The answers will depend on cultural and social factors, reflecting the family's environment and experiences, so we give no prescriptions of behavior. We simply offer ideas on a family

Table **3.1** *Common business family values*

Value	Behavior
Responsibility*	Family First, Business First, or Family Enterprise
Fairness*	Consistency, clarity, communication, changeability, fairness, commitment
Stewardship	Perseverance, long-term, determination, hard work, legacy, responsible
Social responsibility	Do the right thing, honor, trustworthy, reputation, philanthropy, concern, sharing
Respect	Empathy, hierarchy, tolerance, golden rule, compassion, trust, generosity, individuality
Independence	Self determination, thinking, reliability, freedom, expression, hard work
Family connection	Enthusiasm, joy, passion, adventure, celebration, cohesion, support, caring
Leadership	Vision, quality, effectiveness, empowering, values, purpose, power
Entrepreneurship	Opportunities, growth, innovation, new ventures, social entrepreneurship

*Note: Responsibility and Fairness are transcendent values that influence how a business family expresses its other values.

business philosophy and fairness to stimulate the reader's thinking and learning.

Family business responsibilities

Business families struggle with setting priorities. Some families may choose to honor business responsibilities as the highest priority. These Business First families take decisions based on what will be best for the company, its customers, employees, and shareholders. Others take a Family First perspective, considering that the family's satisfaction and connections should come before everything else. We propose a different approach, Enterprising Family Thinking, as a middle ground to balance conflicting responsibilities. Family Enterprise Thinking recognizes that in the real world compromise is required, and that the best solutions are sensitive to the competing needs of all the stakeholders.

Business First families focus on what they do for their business and its stakeholders. This means decisions are based on what will be best for the company, including its customers, employees, and shareholders. Professional business principles are used to govern such matters as employment, compensation, and governance. Such principles can constitute excellent criteria by which to make the tough decisions that will affect the entire family, even if they lead to unequal treatment and feelings of unfairness.

The owner of a UK family business that employs over 15,000 workers in the service sector says,

> We think that our most important responsibility is protecting our employees' jobs and benefits. The employees make our success possible and deserve full consideration. The law sets the minimum wage but we want to invest in our people's future so we are more productive, and hence a stronger competitor.

Family First families have a very different focus. Their founders often create businesses with the intention of providing for the ones they love and – if they are successful – creating a better life for them all. Starting a business can be a hardship for such families, as the founder's time, money, and talent are invested in the firm. However, these sacrifices can create strong feelings of family connection and psychological ownership. Family First decisions may favor family happiness, equality, and unity, even if they come at some expense to the company's future success.

The owner of a US engineering business says,

> My family invested their lives in supporting me and this business, and my primary responsibility is to take care of every family member and be ready to provide financial assistance if there's a crisis or if they need it. It is my personal commitment to them.

Enterprising Family Thinking is focused on the family, business, *and* stakeholders. This third model expands the definition of the family's focus beyond the operating businesses, and includes a family office and foundation, as well as other family ventures, as part of a larger enterprise. This philosophy holds that plans and decisions must provide for both the family's satisfaction and the business' performance. Its balanced approach creates a family commitment that can sustain future ownership. Family members who hold this view believe that neglecting the needs of either family or business will threaten the future. They have a long-term commitment to the future of the business and the family – and are required to resolve conflicts between the two creatively.

The owner of a family business in South America says:

> Our family is blessed compared to others and that creates a stewardship responsibility. Our focus is on heavy investment to build a sustainable business that meets the needs of all our stakeholders, communities and creates family wealth. Through our wages and purchasing we make a big difference to our entire community but that is not enough. Every year, 15 percent of the dividends are transferred to the family foundation that my two daughters direct to support a wide range of charities.

As discussed earlier, clarifying the family's responsibilities helps set the stage for resolving the many decisions that are likely to arouse conflict. While every family must decide what is best for it, we suggest that consideration be given to the Enterprise Family doctrine. Table 3.2 summarizes possible family business decisions using the three different models as criteria. Table 3.2 details how different business philosophies affect decisions common to all family businesses. When deciding who will be allowed to join the family business, the Business First model selects only those offspring who meet the highest employment criteria, such as academic qualifications and work experience. The Family First model provides jobs for all family members. And the Family Enterprise model offers a blended approach valuing the family member's interest and his or her qualifications for the job.

In such situations balancing family and business goals requires clear values, careful planning, and regular communication. The reason for discussing and agreeing on a family business philosophy is to guide the family's planning and decision making on business policies and family agreements. Once the family's thinking on responsibilities and priorities has been clarified, the next step is a discussion of the conditions under which the family will work together to ensure fairness.

Table 3.2 *Family business philosophy as a guideline for decision making*

Decision	Business First	Family First	Family Enterprise
Employment	Business need and qualifications	Family welcome	Family interest and qualifications
Compensation	Market rate	Equal	Market rate with adjustments by family
Ownership	Stock options based on contribution	Family decision	Family decision with stock options possible
Roles and authority	Roles and authority based on position description	Shared roles e.g. all director title, shared decision making	Roles and authority based on position description with family communication
Governance	Board with a majority of outside directors	Family-dominated board	Board with outside and family directors and a family council
Goals	Financial performance	Family satisfaction	Stewardship
Dividends	Small with large reinvestment	Large	Variable and significant reinvestment

Fairness builds engagement and contribution, and it is hoped will lead to long-term family commitment. It also helps family members to discuss how shared values can make an impact on their shared future.

Family fairness

One of the universal challenges for families is dealing with issues of justice or fairness. Interpersonal relationships and cultural norms about respect and hierarchy shape what is perceived as fair. In most families one of the first responses a child makes to his or her parents when they disagree with a decision or outcome is "It's not fair." In the family business setting this is amplified because striving for equality between siblings and cousins is a lifelong activity. And "It's not fair" is transferred from the playground to the boardroom.

Business families are faced with fairness in every aspect of planning and decision making for the family and firm. Family businesses are at the same time the place where fairness is most needed, and yet where it is most difficult to achieve. Is it fair for the first-born son to be named the CEO because of his birth position in the family? Is it fair to divide the shares among all the family shareholders equally, knowing some do not care about the business while others are passionate about it? Is it fair to promote family members who are not the most competent to executive positions?

The adolescent and young adult years are known for conflicts and struggles between parents and their children. Parents want control; kids want independence. The fairness dilemmas that many families have are a residual effect of unresolved parent–child relationships. A behavior pattern evolves as parents exercise control over their children's lives to insure their safety and development. Even after the children become adults, this parental role remains a part of the family's scripts and structure, and the next generation remains "children" as long as their parents are alive.

Businesses are also organized around a hierarchy based on roles and authority. The management and shareholders make decisions that direct the business and its strategy. Successful performance reinforces this structure and its processes – but sometimes to the detriment of the next generation. Such rigid structure means younger family members cannot express new ideas or aspirations without challenging the management's proven formula for success. This limits their participation and chance to experience a sense of personal autonomy.

Family Fair Process

One approach for dealing with fairness that we have run has worked very well. Family relationships based on trust created by Fair Process set the stage for effective dialog and decision making. Fair Process consists of a set of behaviors that create transparency so that all family members recognize why and how decisions are made. It does not, however, guarantee that the outcome will be fair.[8]

The fact that family relationships last a lifetime should be a powerful motivation for practicing fairness. Family firms are built on successful personal relationships that become a competitive advantage only if they can engage and focus the family's talents and commitment. Harry McNeely, Jr., whose family was split by a bitter shareholder dispute (see Chapter 9), recalls how a perceived lack of fairness created his family's conflicts:

> When I think about it, my parents tried very hard to be fair. But my sisters didn't feel that way. In terms of money, perhaps they had been treated more than fairly. But emotionally they felt that the division hadn't been fair. My father felt strongly that men belonged in business and women in the household. He wouldn't be perceived as a modern thinker.

Most business families discuss fairness as part of their family values, but we would argue that Fair Process is more than a value. It is an approach to working together.[9] Without question, one of the most common problems arising in family businesses is a lack of communication. The goal of Fair Process goes beyond fairness to improving family communication, by institutionalizing listening and information sharing about critical issues like ownership, policies, and values.

The rationale is simple. Individuals are most likely to trust and cooperate freely with systems – whether they themselves win or lose by those systems – when Fair Process is observed. At first glance Fair Process may seem like a Western solution to building family harmony, but its principles work in a wide range of cultural contexts because it is about *how* we make decisions, not *who* makes decisions. Remember, however, that adopting Fair Process as a family behavior does not necessarily reduce the authority of the senior generation. The owners are still the owners, but Fair Process ensures the next generation takes a part in decision making. Participating in decisions creates an environment where family members learn about the business and feel an engagement that supports the family's actions.

Fair Process, as already mentioned, does not ensure that outcomes are always fair. Fair Process stipulates, for example, that the family needs to agree – after discussion and sharing relevant information – what policy it will use for hiring family members. This policy should then be applied consistently to all family members. Applying Fair Process helps a family prevent conflict between siblings because it establishes an internal family justice for career decisions. The general concept of family Fair Process is built on five principles:

- *Communication* is allowing a voice to all family members.
- *Clarity* is sharing accurate and timely information with the family.
- *Consistency* is uniformly applying agreements to all members.
- *Changeability* is being willing to change rules as situations change.
- *Culture of fairness* is committing to Fair Process because it benefits the family through better decisions.

Fair Process acknowledges that families and businesses are not democracies, and that certain members have more influence and control over the final decisions. It can mean that the entrepreneur and controlling shareholder who decides his oldest son will succeed him as CEO does not need to consult with others in the family or business. Yet it also suggests that – if he wants to ensure family support for his son, strengthen family relationships, and consider all options for sound decision making – he should listen to and fully consider the family's opinions. And, after accepting the new input he should also explain his decision to the family. This is often a difficult change in behavior for family and business leaders to make, but it is a critical step in ensuring the contribution of the family's emotional and intellectual talent to the business. The decision may turn out to be the same as without Fair Process, but the family's commitment to the decision could be very different.

The application of Fair Process reflects the family's culture and environment, as the members work to create fairness in their dealings with each other, the business, and its stakeholders. The Murugappa family mentioned earlier has developed a Bill of Rights for their male family members around key themes: the right to question and seek clarifi-

Figure 3.7 *Comparing family business responsibilities*

Murugappa Bill of Rights: Each Male Family Member

Has the right to be given an opportunity to work in any of the Group companies provided he has an aptitude for the job.

Has the right to get a salary commensurate with the level of responsibility held and performance in the business.

Has the right to question (or seek clarification) with regard to any decision that, in his opinion, will/may affect the Group--with clear understanding that he will abide by the majority decision of the family members.

Has the right to have information on any major happening (event) that takes place in the Group e.g. acquisition, closure, collaboration, etc.

Has the right to a certain reasonable standard of living and to be provided with the necessities to maintain such standard.

Has the right to pursue a career of his choice and not be bound to work in the Murugappa Group. In such event he has the right to maintain his share of business and other assets without being involved in the management.

---

cation; the right to information, the right to ownership; and the right to a career based on aptitude (see Figure 3.7). Fair Process, because it reflects the family's unique context, must be culturally sensitive. The points identified in the Murugappa Bill of Rights are not exactly the same as five principles of Fair Process described above, but they serve the same purpose of guiding the family's interactions. It is also important to recognize – even if it is something that Western readers cannot fully accept – that in many Indian families daughters are considered part of their husband's family, so are not covered by their family's bill of rights.

Balancing family and business responsibilities in a manner that is perceived as fair by the family is a significant step toward clarifying the family's values. This approach helps the family start to work together in new ways that improve both communication and effectiveness. Once the family has agreed on how to balance its responsibilities and work together to create a sense of fairness, the family is prepared to explore the values that will drive its plans and vision.

IDENTIFYING YOUR FAMILY VALUES

The *Parallel Planning Process* begins with business families agreeing on their shared values as the foundation for planning and investment, which will lead in turn to an agreement on the family's commitment to the business. Talking about values is important because – as we have seen in this chapter – the family's values are the foundation of meaningful family and business actions. It is easy to talk, of course, but this is the vital first step in moving from espoused to enacted values. A shared family value about long-term investment, for example, can become a family agreement on a dividend policy resulting in a 70 percent reinvestment of profits in the business. However, turning abstract values into real actions in this way is not always easy.

A series of family meetings may be required to identify a list of values, discuss why they are important, and then focus on a few values that will serve as the basis for the family's business practices and family relationships. Family values can mean different things to different individuals – so it is important to allow time for discussion, reflection, and negotiation to develop consensus on not only what the family values are, but also how they are reflected in planning and action. Developing an understanding of core values is particularly important when multiple generations of a family or in-laws become involved with the business. All will have different experiences and agendas, hence potentially different interpretations of the family's values, than the current senior generation.

Families can approach identifying shared values in many different ways. One typical method is for the discussion to evolve through a series of task-force meetings. The interdependence of the family system means that the beliefs and actions of each individual influence the other members. Thus – if a family has good communication skills and works well together – one simple way to begin is to ask each family member to share a value they feel contributes to the family's success. The different answers from around the table are recorded on a flip chart, stimulating meaningful – and possibly even heated – discussion. The family can then rationalize similar results and work to develop a consensus on the key values. It is important to allow sufficient time for everyone to express their ideas and respond to others. It may be necessary first to identify core values that everyone agrees on, then to put other values on the agenda for future family meetings.

Other approaches may be equally powerful. Some families use a more historical method, and find sharing stories about the family business' great successes and failures are a powerful tool for capturing the family's values. This approach is less abstract, and helps to identify examples of behaviors and actions that pass from one generation to another. It can also take the form of a social event where meaningful anecdotes are exchanged. However, the next step is again a discussion aimed at understanding the underlying message. What were the values embedded in that story? And what does it mean to our family?

Larger families, with multiple generations, may need to need to ask for help from outsiders, especially if their involvement in the business has diminished over recent years. The contribution of outsiders to the process of value identification can be very helpful. The family can ask trusted non-family executives or board members, or even key customers, who have known the business and family for a long time, about their perspectives. Outsiders who know the family well are often able to pinpoint the family's values more accurately and with more meaningful language than the family might use itself. This can also be a bonding experience for members of the next generation, who can interview people connected with the family as part of the process. They can even develop a "stakeholder map" of what people and communities who have a stake in the family business think about the family's values. Family businesses tend to have longer, stronger, and more personal stakeholder relationships than other firms. Starting the exploration of family values by analyzing the family's impact on others thus encourages a long-term perspective and –ultimately – planning that will benefit all stakeholders rather than just focusing on the family and its expectations.

The overlap of the family and business systems turns many routine questions about stakeholders into questions about values. We have identified several examples:

- honoring obligations created by previous generations to employees, customers, or vendors
- treating all employees equitably regarding compensation and rewards
- making only reasonable work or time demands
- providing career development opportunities for non-family and family employees
- committing to using merit and performance as criteria in promotions

- demanding the same standards of conduct and behavior from family and non-family employees
- addressing the issue of family members' performance
- keeping family conflicts out of the workplace.

Some families find that discussing values is too difficult. Instead they may find it helpful to discuss concrete behaviors and then identify their underlying family values. Figure 3.8 suggests a list of open-ended statements that can stimulate thinking about how the family's values affect family business success and challenges. These questions are also useful in outlining topics for inclusion in the discussion of Family Agreements (discussed in Chapters 8 and 9).

Figure 3.8 *Statements on family business values*

Values Discussion Exercise
Successful families always …
Our family legacy is …
Our most important priority as a family is …
Someone who wants to be influential in our family must …
Balancing my personal life and career will …
Our family has a responsibility to ensure that …
When faced with a family conflict, our family …
When faced with a business challenge our family …
Our family is blessed with success because …

The first meetings about values are not likely to be easy or polite. But if the family takes its job seriously, this will be an honest process that develops family communication skills and a better mutual understanding. The important outcome is that – as the family explores its core values – many ideas related to family commitment will start to emerge.

The importance of making the family's values an important part of the decision-making and planning process is well captured by Dr. Peter Zinkann, former co-managing director of Miele & Cie. GmbH in Germany in a letter to his successor.[10] He instructs his protégé:

What is the essence of Miele? At first glance it is quality – our credo that quality comes first, and everything else comes second. At second glance I believe the essence of Miele is love. Not only Rudolf Miele's love for the company and my love for the company, but also the love that the vast majority of our employees bring to their work and to Miele.

FAMILY BUSINESS CULTURE

Culture is the business' expression of its values. Businesses do not have values like families because they are composed of individuals whose only affiliation is organizational. A business culture develops when these individuals share organizational experiences (success and failure) to institutionalize a shared set of beliefs and assumptions about how they work together effectively to achieve their goals.[11] These beliefs and assumptions become a tool that aligns divergent attitudes and behaviors about both social and technical organizational tasks. As Pier Giuseppe Beretta states in *The World of Beretta*, "Culture is in the walls here. It becomes part of you with each breath. There is a certain something that is common to everyone in this company, something shared, yet unspoken."

It is important to consider a business' culture as a part of planning because – like the family's values – it shapes employee thinking, decision making, strategy, and implementation. Consider Xerox. Despite inventing the computer mouse, the company did not manufacture or market the product because the organization's culture was not cognitively open. It was an office products company and it didn't see how this new invention was an office product. Xerox sold the technology to Apple, and it became the heart of a strategy supporting a more user-friendly approach to personal computing.

The topic of business culture is widely discussed in the management literature, and our intention here is limited to exploring the connection between family values and family business culture. McKinsey, the consulting group, has developed a model, based on the work of R. T. Pascale and A. G. Athos in their book *The Art of Japanese Management*, that we find useful for business families. The basic premise of the model is that organizations have seven key activities that need to be aligned if the firm is to be successful. Three are technical tasks: strategy, structure, and systems. Four are social tasks: shared values (culture), style, staff, and skills.

Figure 3.9 *Description of the 7S organization factors*

Organizational Factors

Strategy is the company's formula for creating value by matching the firm's capabilities with market opportunities.

Style is the way people act and relate to each other.

Structure is the organization's reporting relationships and functions.

Systems is the processes to complete tasks and support the flow of information.

Staff is the type of people.

Skills are the key competencies and capabilities required for the execute the business strategy.

Shared values is the culture that creates the implicit rules for how people behave.

The McKinsey model demonstrates how organizational performance is related to the aligment of shared values (culture) and structure, strategy, systems, style, staff, and skills. Their work with consulting clients has shown that organization effectiveness is influenced by the interconnection and interdependence of the variables. In simple terms each of the factors influences the other and must support the other. This model assumes that shared values (culture) reflect why the organization exists and what factors make it successful (see Figure 3.10 below).

Figure 3.10 *The 7S model of organizational alignment for performance*

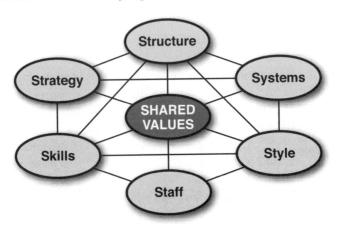

Source: McKinsey Mind Tools.com, "Enduring Ideas: The 7-S Framework."

Family-business culture is a particularly powerful tool for motivating individual and organizational performance and creating behavioral norms that support the firm's strategy. The advantage of a strong culture is that it empowers employees and reduces management's dependence on administrative controls or sanctions like policies, procedures, budgets, and employee performance reviews.

A good example of the effectiveness of cultural versus administrative controls is found in the financial services industry, where the recent economic downturn forced many large banks to be merged or sold. It is generally accepted that the much of this economic malaise was self-inflicted by the large banks and their employees, who – despite extensive administrative controls – maximized short-term gains for their own advantage. A comparison of the large publicly traded banks and their family business peers demonstrates the impact of family cultures on performance. The family-controlled banks (including Banco Santander, Julius Baer Group, C. Hoare & Co., Pictet & Cie, and Lombard Odier Darier Hentsch & Cie) have experienced fewer asset write-offs and are strengthening their market positions. One important reason is the family firms' commitment to a culture based on long-term performance and accountability. They did not chase the quick profits because they preferred to plan and invest for the long term. Their strong cultures supported organizations where employees, management, directors, and owners were all focused on building their businesses, not their bonuses.

Family businesses often use the different aspects of the firm's culture such as value statements, visions, myths, and stories as management tools to shape employee behavior. Large and publicly traded firms tend to rely on policies, procedures, reviews, and audits to ensure employee compliance. The finance literature shows that family-controlled firms outperform other comparable firms on the S&P 500. We believe there are four possible explanations, all connected to values.

- *Tenure and stability*: Family businesses tend to have more stability and longer tenure of leadership.
- *History*: Family businesses tend to be constantly in touch with their history and their legacy.
- *Family values*: The culture of family businesses tends to be more durable, more powerful, and more meaningful to the organization than for non-family businesses.

■ *More positive beliefs*: Management teams in family businesses tend to have much more positive beliefs about human nature than those in non-family businesses.

WHEN FAMILY BUSINESSES ARE BEST

■ Values are a guide to decision making and can be a source of competitive advantage to a family business.
■ Family values can address a wide range of themes or topics to provide a source of strength and continuity.
■ As the family and company grow, values need to be shared among the family and employees. The best family businesses work hard to communicate their values throughout the family business system.
■ Fair Process is also a tool for strengthening family communication and relationships, allowing families to make better decisions and plans that reflect the aspirations of the entire family.

4 Family and Business Vision: Exploring Family Commitment

Family Actions

Business Actions

"We will build stores in small, rural towns-skipping the major cities-and overtake Sears within 30 years." When Sam Walton uttered these words to a small group of trusted employees, few people outside of Arkansas believed that Walmart had much of a chance of displacing Sears as the world's largest retailer. But what others thought didn't matter because Sam was concerned about encouraging his employees and family to believe in something bigger than a handful of stores. He knew his innovative strategy of building big stores in small towns would capture market share if his team believed in it. His vision became the criterion for measuring all of their decisions: does this action support us in becoming the largest retailer in the world?

Walmart is not alone. One characteristic of long-lasting successful organizations is that they are driven by powerful visions that help them overcome their daily struggles, problems, and conflicts to focus on the future. Miyamoto Musashi, the Japanese military strategist, captured this important benefit of a vision in his treatise, *The Book of Five Rings* (1645): "If one fixes one's concentration on minor matters, one loses sight of major concerns, and causes one to lose opportunities for a sure victory." This vision process is a valuable tool for helping business families focus their attention on new possibilities and opportunities in a world of "minor matters."

We all know and remember meaningful visions because they instill a desire for belonging and contributing. They make us admire what is being attempted and want to participate actively.[1] The three visions below by Martin Luther King, Winston Churchill, and John F. Kennedy respectively remain classics for their appeal and simplicity.

- I have a dream . . .
- We will fight on the beaches . . .
- A man on the moon by 1970 . . .

"We will change the way people, learn, work and play" is an equally memorable vision from the world of business. One could argue that an important reason for Steve Jobs' and Apple's success is that this vision broadened the application of technology beyond a work tool to become a part of all aspects of our lives. It pervaded their product design, marketing, stores, and services by rejecting the previous paradigm that technology was for the experts not the masses. The Apple vision became the criterion by which Jobs and his team shaped a company, which – by its unusual name, logo, and market position – said technology could be simple, friendly, fun, and useful all at the same time.

The family business vision statement is the family and its stakeholders' shared agreement on a desired future state, as defined by their values. The family's vision expresses a shared commitment to the business and family's future success. It is what they want to become by working together. The vision statement is anchored in the future, usually five to ten or more years ahead, and includes a vivid description of the positive outcomes expected. Visions call for action and are inclusive so that they invite commitment from the entire organization. Effective family business visions support the family's commitment because they are:

- meaningful – to support consensus on tough decisions
- engaging – to encourage talent development
- future-focused – to support long-term actions

■ authentic – to match the family's values
■ challenging – to support new possibilities.

Developing and using a shared vision is important to family businesses: it is a part of their identity, of who they are. Entrepreneurial founders seldom think about selling the business. Yet inevitably, every successful entrepreneur will have to hand over the reins, transferring leadership and ownership to the next generation. Often the next generation will have very different motivations – its commitment to the business is by no means guaranteed. In most cases continued family ownership is assumed even if the family or business situation has changed. However, selling may be an appropriate action in some cases.

Discussing the family vision and commitment is at best difficult because most families espouse a commitment to continued ownership without thinking carefully about the family's investment, the business' potential or the family's expectations. Even assuming that each individual has the same level of commitment as the founders, group behavior and communication challenges make it less likely that commitment will be clearly expressed – and acted upon – in a forceful way. Powerful family business visions are the link in the *Parallel Planning Process* between family values and strategy, investment and governance planning.

A meaningful shared vision encourages commitment especially during generational transitions, giving family firms an important tool to align family and business planning for the future. Shanti Poesposo-etjipto, head of the Soedarpo family office and chair of PT Samudera Indonesia Tbk in Indonesia, captures the power of a shared vision that supported her family:

> The family has a destiny. The company has a destiny. It's a blessing if you can keep them as one – but there's no guarantee. When my father died, many people came and asked if the company was for sale. But we didn't even consider it.

THE FAMILY VISION AND BUILDING FAMILY COMMITMENT

The family business vision supports family commitment, and without family commitment to drive planning and action, the vision is nothing more than a dream or aspiration. All family businesses need a strong commitment from their stakeholders, especially the owners. A well-recognized study of commitment describes it as follows:

> Commitment supposes something beyond mere passing loyalty to an organization. It involves an active relationship with the organization such that individuals are willing to give something of themselves in order to contribute to the organization's well being.[2]

This active relationship and giving of family talents and resources is what sets family businesses apart and creates a competitive advantage over non-family firms.

The importance of aligning the family, owners, board, and management around a shared vision may sound obvious, but we see many cases where different stakeholders are working from different road maps of the business' future (see Figure 4.1). The management team will have budgets and action plans; the board will have a strategic plan; and the family will have ownership and participation expectations – but the family vision should encompass all of these. It is particularly serious if the owners cannot agree among themselves about the future of the business. When this happens, the management and the board are frustrated and there is a general lack of focus on new strategies or activities. Many of the damaging family business conflicts discussed in the media exemplify this situation. Business families may struggle to

Figure 4.1 *Family vision as the North Star*

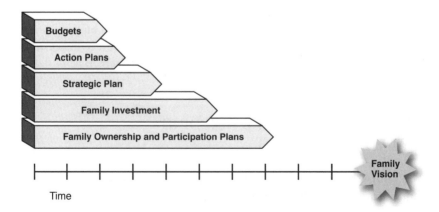

develop a shared vision but there are many benefits to be derived from the process, which can:

- provide a "guiding star" for family decisions
- describe how the family can contribute to the business' success
- require learning and working as a family team
- help new generations to develop and own plans
- represent the family's collective commitment to each other
- strengthen and renew the family's values, rituals and traditions.

Each family business needs to craft its own unique vision. A vision statement may include or mention the family's values, goals, mission, strategy, and even governance, but what really matters is engaging the family and their key stakeholders (whether customers, non-family owners, employees, or others). The style and scope of the vision will also reflect each family business' situation. However, just like values, discussed in Chapter 3, the family business vision will have an impact on all parts of the family business system.

We will examine three family business visions, each with a different focus:

- the Kanoo vision, which focuses on the family and their community
- the Estée Lauder vision, which focuses on a Fortune 500 firm's relationship with its customers
- the McNeely family vision, which focuses on how the family contributes to the business' success.

The Kanoo, Lauder, and McNeely family businesses are different in their size, complexity, market, culture, ownership, and history, so it is only logical that their vision statements reflect these differences. The Kanoos are from Bahrain and their business is the oldest of the three; Estée Lauder is New York Stock Exchange traded and global; the McNeely business is regional and owned by six American siblings and their father.

LEGACY-FOCUSED VISION

The 120-year-old Kanoo family business, one of the Middle East's oldest, integrates values and future aspirations into its vision statement. The Kanoo family vision is driven by four values: fairness, support, respect, and community – ideals that they believe support family unity and business success. Vision, values, and strategies are combined seamlessly to create a powerful statement that provides the family business system with a shared view of the future (see Figure 4.2). The vision transmits values about profitability, but the Kanoos are clearly just as focused on social responsibility as on new markets or business opportunities.

Figure 4.2 *Legacy-focused vision*

Kanoo Family Vision

Preserves the good name of the Yusuf Bin Ahmed Kanoo family

Creates and sustains family wealth

Creates a world-class enterprise operating with the highest levels of integrity

Unites the family and creates a legacy which the family can be proud of

Is a good employer and attracts and nurtures the best people, be they family or non-family

Acts philanthropically and serves the community within which it operates

---

Khalid Kanoo, a senior family leader and founder of the Bahrain Family Business Association, sees another important benefit to the family from clarifying its vision:

> Many family businesses create a terrible family legacy of unhappiness and destruction. If the family does not prepare the children for wealth their goal can become enjoying the money without concern for their responsibilities. The family needs to teach the next generation about taking care of the business, family and community.

BUSINESS-FOCUSED VISION

Estée Lauder, one of the world's leading manufacturers and marketers of quality skin care, make-up, fragrance, and hair care products, generates annual sales of over US$7 billion. Its products are sold in markets around the world and include many well-recognized brand names. Its business vision demonstrates the power of an external focus on marketplace and customers. The

Estée Lauder Companies Inc. guiding vision is simply: "Bringing the best to everyone we touch." And that means the best products, the best people, and the best ideas. These three pillars have been the hallmarks of the company since Estée Lauder founded it in 1946.

A good example of how the vision of touching customers' lives drives the organization beyond sales and profits is the Pink Ribbon activities of the Estée Lauder Companies' Breast Cancer Awareness Campaign. This global effort, reaching across cultures and languages, is driven by the Lauder family's vision of serving its customers beyond cosmetics to create "a world without breast cancer." The size of the business – and the fact that it is widely traded (despite being family controlled) – demands a business vision that influences marketing, management, and even philanthropy.

FAMILY-FOCUSED VISION

The McNeely family has created a family-centered vision for the Meritex Corporation, a leading US warehousing and distribution firm. This fourth-generation business involves a father and his six children as shareholders – the oldest son is CEO and chairman, the father (now in his eighties) serves as chairman emeritus, and three family members are on the board of directors. The family has had a turbulent history, experiencing two major business conflicts over the last 75 years (discussed in Chapter 9). As a result, the family business was split after a lawsuit between the founder's four children and again when two of them (one of whom is the current chairman emeritus) could not agree on a shared vision regarding family ownership and participation.

The current McNeely family team has made its shared vision a fundamental part of planning and governance activities. The vision statement explicitly mentions "a loving and united family that celebrates our values of integrity, compassion and respect," reflecting a family which has lived through the consequences of unsolved conflicts and is determined not to repeat the experience (see Figure 4.3). The vision confirms a family committed to protecting its members and working together as stewards to support the business' future success. The statement has been revised several times over the last ten years to reflect changes in the family's role and to prepare the fourth generation of McNeelys for active ownership.

The McNeely family vision, though relatively short, contains a significant amount of information about the family's intentions for its business and itself. This family's values drive a vision of responsibility and capable ownership. The statement stresses the importance of stewardship and clearly articulates the family members' planned future for their business and their expectations for themselves. It clarifies the family's and the board's responsibilities to the

Figure 4.3 *Family-focused vision*

McNeely Family Business Vision

As the shareholders and stewards of Meritex Enterprises we will act from a multi-generational perspective to enhance our financial and emotional investment in the Company. The shareholders will be represented by a board of directors whose duty is to grow the company and enhance our interests as well as those of our customers, employees, and its communities. Meritex's success is founded on the competitive advantage its knowledge, operating skills and financial strength provide customers.

---

business – and to each other for ensuring performance and asset growth. The statement strongly emphasizes the role of the board of directors because the lack of an effective governance structure led to many of their past disputes, and the eventual lawsuit that resulted in the company and family split. The vision statement also articulates the family's responsibilities to a "multi-generation perspective, being informed and objective and fiscally responsible." In short, the vision summarizes the family participation, strategy and governance processes.

There is no doubt among the Kanoos, Lauders, or McNeelys about the families' commitment to supporting their businesses. The three visions reflect different focuses, as the businesses are different in terms of ownership, demographics, and culture. But all the families are united as long-term supporters of their businesses in terms of contributing financial and human capital.

DRAFTING A FAMILY BUSINESS VISION

So far, everything sounds good, but how does a family start creating a family vision? The first informal family vision emerges out of the founder's aspirations for his or her business. There was no doubt what Estée Lauder had in mind when she created the cosmetics company that bears her name. Typically, the more formal family vision statement flows out of discussions about family values and answers the question: What do we want our family business to become in the future, and how does the family contribute? This vision depends on the intentions of a group of family members; it is influenced by the business' potential and the family's values, expectations, and commitment (see Figure 4.4). Family values are fundamental because values express what is important to us. Talking about them naturally stimulates discussions about vision – and vice versa. For example, a vision of "a business that lasts forever" is heavy with values about long-term thinking, family connections, and ownership responsibilities.

Vision discussions can focus either on business aspirations or on family aspirations, because the two systems are interrelated. As the CEO of the Merck Group, a family-controlled global German pharmaceutical firm, commented when it received the 2009 IMD Family Business of the Year Award in Amsterdam, "If the family has a vision, then the business has a vision." No matter what approach is used, the family business vision developed will reflect the family's values about what is important in its shared future. Again regardless of approach, serious family discussions will be required about the variables in Figure 4.4 with a view to developing family consensus by exploring different family members' perspectives. Four questions that can help business shape a vision are:

- What family values support continued ownership and investment in the business? (Discussed in Chapter 3.)
- What is the business' potential to create value for the family and stakeholders (business potential)?

Figure 4.4 *The factors influencing family business vision*

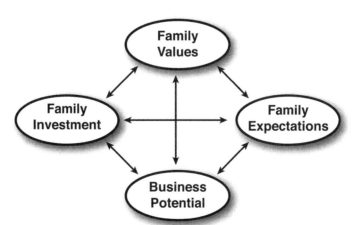

- What do the family owners expect from the business (family expectations)?
- How does the family add value for the business (family investment)?

To ask these four questions is to recognize that the family's vision is related and interdependent with these factors. A business with high potential needs a family whose values, investment, and expectations are aligned and mutually supportive. Family vision, like everything to do with family businesses, requires discussion, thinking, and planning.

Business potential

The question regarding value creation is one of basic economics and psychology. The business needs to create value for the family in the form of good financial returns and/or strong psychological rewards (like supporting the family's reputation). If there is no good return on the family's investment of its financial and human capital, then the family either needs a plan to regenerate the business, or it needs to begin thinking about a harvest-or-sell strategy. The business world of the twenty-first century is too competitive to struggle to keep an unprofitable business with a weak future alive. The assessment of the business' strategic potential is further discussed in Chapter 6 so that readers can make informed decisions about their investments.

Family expectations

We call the answer to the third of our questions the "shareholders' value proposition," as it identifies what family owners would like from their family investment. Factors such as the business' market, characteristics, possible returns, capital structure, and growth rate are possible criteria (see Figure 4.5). These can be used to make decisions about the existing business or new business decisions or investments. For example, if the current family business is in a mature market with a low growth rate, the shareholders' value proposition articulates the family's expectations from the business and – when combined with the family values statement – begins to define the family's thinking about its future vision for both family and business. Many families find that discussing the concrete expectations of shareholders adds a sense of

Figure 4.5 *Family expectations*

Shareholder Value Proposition

Business characteristics (industry, products, markets served)

Business diversification (Product or brand extensions)

Level and sources of risk (technology, competition, regulation)

Investment required and debt structure

Returns: liquidity, dividends, and capital gains

Growth rate and profitability

Long-term prospects and sustainability

Family benefits (jobs, offices, networks)

reality to the process of developing a vision, a concept that often seems rather abstract – and which George Bush, Sr. famously dismissed as "the vision thing."

Family investment

Our fourth and critical question is about the family's willingness to invest human capital (family talent) and financial capital (money) to contribute to the business' future success. We see this investment as the truest measure of a business family's commitment to the firm. If family members say that business ownership is important, what investments are they making to support these values? A family that expects a large dividend will be able to support a very different strategy from a family that reinvests 90 percent of the firm's earnings back into the business. The first family uses up capital, while the second creates a competitive advantage by being a source of investment capital. To answer the question about investment is ultimately to set the stage for a serious discussion of whether the family is committed to long-term ownership.

Should we own this business?

An early premise of the academic field of family business was that family ownership should always be continued. Ownership continuity became the measure of success without concern for other types of economic, emotional, or social impact on the family. Yet it is by no means obvious that business ownership should always be transferred within the family. In reality, it might be best for all concerned if the business were to be sold. A weak business in a mature market, a lack of family commitment or a chronic conflict may make it unwise for the family to maintain ownership. Discussion can be difficult because the sensitive questions that the family must ask about its commitment may never have been fully addressed. In addition, family commitment is a subjective topic with no clear criteria to support its exploration.

We have therefore developed a simple model that many families find useful for discussing family vision and commitment. It uses the family's financial investment as a measure of commitment. The decision of dividends versus reinvestment occurs regularly, and requires a concrete decision from the family or board. In simple terms, as we saw above, if we compare two families with similar businesses, a family that is taking 90 percent of the profits as dividends or family payouts is expressing a different ownership commitment than a family that is plowing 90 percent back into the business.

Our framework identifies four possible investment strategies: *invest, hold, harvest,* and *sell* (see Figure 4.6). The first two strategies, *invest* and *hold,* involve investment in the business and sustaining the family's future ownership, while the last two, *harvest* and *sell,* suggest liquidity and reducing the family's ownership position. The investment decision is discussed further in Chapter 7, but the four possible investment strategies can be summarized as follows:

- *invest:* a fully committed family (or strong subset of the family) opting for continued financial investment
- *hold:* a family seeking continued investment but deciding to buy out one or more owners or to reduce its new investment through a joint venture
- *harvest:* a family intending to create liquidity or reduce its ownership position through private equity or by listing on a stock exchange
- *sell:* a family that is liquidating its entire investment in its operating company or companies.

Figure 4.6 *Family business investment strategies*

INVEST	HOLD			HARVEST	SELL
Investing owners	Joint venture	Internally buyout selected owners	Private equity buyout	Public offering	Sell business

CARGILL: BALANCING FAMILY VALUES, EXPECTATIONS, INVESTMENT, AND BUSINESS POTENTIAL

The interaction of family values, expectations, investment, and business potential is demonstrated in the story of the Cargill family, which struggled with the decision to continue substantially reinvesting in the company versus taking larger dividends.[3] Family businesses frequently face ownership issues during generational transitions because younger family members may expect larger dividends or express concern about the business' growth or performance. Cargill, the world's largest agri-business group with over a century of financial success and value creation (as we saw in Chapter 2), faced a challenge when a group of the owners approached management with a request to raise the dividend or buy them out. Instead of rejecting the owners' request, Whitney MacMillan, the last family CEO, worked with the shareholders, the family council, and board to institute a large stock buyback program.

Realizing the competitive advantage of a committed family ownership group, Cargill orchestrated the sale of 17 percent of the family's stake to an employee ownership trust for over US$800 million. This move created liquidity for the family members interested in selling and, equally important, reinforced Cargill's commitment to its employees. Cargill had always encouraged lifetime employment as a core value, and the employee ownership trust was a strong demonstration of that value. The board was also restructured to represent the views of all the key stakeholders – family, independent directors, and management directors (with the management directors representing the employee trust). Following the buyout, the Cargill and MacMillan families still held over 80 percent of the equity, and most important, these remaining shareholders represented a highly committed ownership group.

The discussion about investment is often the start of the family's thinking about a future vision for the business and should not eliminate any options. It should be a chance for the family to explore its challenges, role, and contribution – together. Management's response to the Cargill stock buyback could have been negative, forcing the family members interested in selling to liquidate stock slowly through the family's internal stock market. Instead management and family saw the buyback as an opportunity to create liquidity, support the goal of continued family ownership, establish employee ownership, and strengthen the commitment of the remaining family shareholders – all at the same time.

The family's vision serves to align strategy, investment, and governance activities. This thoughtful analysis creates a family vision that clarifies the family's commitment to doing what is best for the business, its stakeholders, and the family. If the business is not a high priority for the family, meaning the family are not committed to – and capable of – acting as good stewards of the business, it is unlikely that there will be long-term value creation for anyone. This is an important outcome of the *Parallel Planning Process.*

Some may argue that family commitment is not a requirement for sustaining a family business, and that there are many examples of companies that have survived bad management, governance, and ownership thanks to the momentum of a market-leading product. However, the recent growth in global competition, and increasing market and stakeholder demands, make it less likely that a neglected business will continue to create long-term value. The Dow Jones story of Chapter 1 is an example: the company could have continued as a family-controlled firm but the reality was that the business had missed too many opportunities, and faced a future of declining revenues and falling stock price.

Organizing a vision meeting

There are many practical approaches to the process of crafting a vision statement. It starts with all or part of the family. Some families meet in their entirety, some select a family task force, and others use the family council if one exists. The family may want to invite other people to share their thinking and experience at times – the CEO, the board, or family members from another non-competing businesses. This sharing of perspectives begins the process of developing or updating a family business vision. Meaningful family discussions are needed so that family members can reconcile their views and consider the possibilities – from high-potential opportunities demanding active investment to a harvest strategy of more passive involvement. We discuss organizing family meetings of this type in Chapter 9.

One should not underestimate how important it is for a family to develop a vision – especially a family that is financially successful. Families need some long-term goals to stimulate their collective spirit and think beyond the day-to-day tasks of managing a business to create more wealth. Humans experience meaning in their lives when they are challenged to contribute to something larger than meeting their own needs and wants. They look for something in their work that offers a psychological or spiritual reward. A vision of what the family can become creates a purpose that reduces rivalries, empowers individuals and overcomes life's obstacles.

The *Parallel Planning Process* begins with family values and vision, and adds the family variable to complement planning for the business. In a family-owned business the vision will shape all aspects of the business' strategy and the business' future. If the family's vision is not supported by the family's commitment, it will be very difficult for the business to implement its strategy. A future vision shared by the family and the business is a powerful concept for planning because it focuses thinking on future goals rather than on current issues or problems. For families and their businesses, the shared vision is a linkage between the family values and enacted commitment, which expresses their mutual interdependence and the power of their combined efforts.

SUSTAINING FAMILY COMMITMENT

As business families grow and mature, they all face the challenge of maintaining future generations' interest and commitment to leadership and ownership. Successful business families understand that they need to plan activities that help their members appreciate and experience committed relationships with the firm. In family businesses there are a series of activities that engage the family by addressing the needs and interests of different members – not just to sustain commitment but also to improve effective family functioning. Some family members may not have a strong interest in the business but are concerned about philanthropy or financial investments. These interests are possible tools to keep the support of family members not directly involved in the business but concerned about protecting and building the family's legacy.

Many activities that business families need to support as a part of their family, business, and governance planning also create opportunities to strengthen family commitment. The larger the family, the business, and the wealth, the greater the structures and processes required to meet the family's management and governance responsibilities. Table 4.1 summarizes the main methods of building a diverse family commitment around a wide range of activities beyond the operating business. These activities will be discussed in the next two chapters, but are highlighted here because they support thinking about vision and commitment.

Commitment can be a tricky issue and a source of individual uncertainty and stress, because most family members feel some kind of psychological ownership with the family business. Growing up with a family business can create strong bonds that are difficult to break. Family members who choose not to commit their careers or who are not invited to participate in the business may sense they are losing their connections to the family itself. Conversely, if an individual's strongest link to their family is through the business, he or she might be reluctant to terminate that relationship even if it is not in his or her best long-term interest. That is why it is so important for the family to ensure that members not working for the business have others ways to participate. Mary-Ann Tsao of the Singapore based Tsao family shares her experience:

> I ended up returning to Asia and working for the family foundation that my grandmother started – as opposed to the business itself. As it's devoted to the health of the older generation there was a perfect fit with my skills as a public health physician – skills which are still in short supply in Singapore.

The family's active commitment as responsible owners is critical if the firm is to remain competitive in the market. Private ownership can occasionally have the adverse effect of shielding non-performing firms from the public scrutiny and market pressures that face publicly traded companies. When family owners are active, they are more likely to keep a sharp eye on performance – their own and their competitors' – and avoid falling into the trap of complacency.

Table 4.1 *Family and business activities to build commitment*

Family activities	Business activities
Family cohesion	***Business cohesion***
■ Treat family members with respect	■ Live the shared values and vision
■ Support individual well-being	■ Support fairness
■ Ensure fairness	
■ Family fun (social events)	***Succession planning***
	■ Develop family and non-family talent
Family planning	■ Coaching and performance reviews
■ Articulate family values and vision	
■ Plan family participation and leadership	***Strategic planning***
	■ Opportunity driven
Estate, wealth and life planning	■ Long-term value creation
■ Clarify estate and ownership intentions	■ People development
■ Discuss trusts, taxes, and health contingencies	***Business governance***
	■ Experienced board of directors
Family governance	■ Accountability for performance
■ Hold family meetings	■ Planned interaction with family
■ Write and ratify family agreements	
■ Develop family leadership processes	***Corporate social responsibility***
	■ Hiring and HR practices
Philanthropy	■ Fair trade sourcing and supply
■ Family giving and involvement	■ Gender and other differences
	■ Community development support
Education and development	■ Sustainable business plans
■ Business and financial literacy	
■ Family business and governance knowledge	
■ Internships and career planning	

If family ownership is to continue, each generation needs to renew its commitment to the business. The natural commitment that a son or daughter feels toward a business created by his or her parents may not be experienced by a grandchild who barely knew the founders. There is also the issue of changing family dynamics and structure. Three siblings can work well together but what happens when there are 24 siblings and half-siblings?

AN ASIAN FAMILY'S STRUGGLE TO RENEW COMMITMENT

The Eu family of Singapore faced a long-term loss of family commitment that developed over two generations.[4] The story was also influenced by war, estate taxes, lack of planning, a large family of 24 children, and the dramatically changing Asian marketplace. At the end of the nineteenth century, Eu Kong, a Chinese tin miner, began a small Chinese herbal medicine company, Eu Yan Sang, to provide for the health of his miners. The practice at the time was to sell the miners morphine to calm them and ease the pain caused by dangerous and physically demanding work. His son, Eu Tong Sen, dramatically expanded the family business, extending the empire to become one of Asia's market leaders in mining, rubber plantations, real estate, and banking.

The Second World War and Eu Tong Sen's death, however, left the Eu family racked by uncertainty, conflict, and legal battles as his 13 sons, from ten wives, struggled for control of the family dynasty. Following the death of the oldest son, the rest of the family accepted that – with the business divided among the 12 surviving sons – it was probably best to pursue their individual business and career interests and slowly sell off the family business units. Tong's death also resulted in devastating double estate tax from both the British and Malaysian governments following the Second World War.

The result was that all of the family companies were sold except the small traditional Chinese medicine business. Despite Eu Yan Sang's meager size, it continued to be a source of long and litigious family disputes, until it was sold to a large conglomerate. In the 1980s, Richard Eu, a member of the fourth generation, joined the firm and began to identify family members who shared a commitment to reviving Eu Yan Sang, based on a vision of rebuilding the business, taking ownership, and stopping their family feuds. Together with his cousins, Joseph and Clifford, Richard organized a leveraged buy out and began developing a new business strategy to regenerate the brand and renew an interest in traditional Chinese medicine.

As the new CEO, Richard demanded a consensus on the family's vision and the owners' commitment as the first step in the planning process, even when this meant "retiring" and buying out his senior family members. The real success factor in Eu Yan Sang was its reformulated vision based on the founder's values of service to others in every aspect of the business. This meant carrying out university research, developing new formulas, marketing to inform people about traditional medicines, and training health professionals. These efforts resulted in a market-leading company that has changed the nature of traditional Chinese medicine. Eu Yan Sang's stores and marketing have won international awards, and its investment in product development and quality control has stimulated a renewed interest in Chinese medicine throughout Asia and the entire Pacific Basin – from Australia to the West Coast of the United States.

The Eu Yan Sang example demonstrates an important outcome of the *Parallel Planning Process* –that is, the use of family values and vision as tools for helping the family confirm (or regain) its commitment to the business. In today's dynamic and global business environment, a committed ownership group is necessary to make a positive contribution to value creation. If a family prefers passive involvement, it may make sense to look at other opportunities, where the family's contribution adds no value. The case of the Bancrofts from the end of Chapter 1 shows the consequences of having a family ownership group that is unable to contribute to the business' governance or strategy.

The development of the family business vision is also the input into the next phases of the *Parallel Planning Process*, creating the link between values on the one hand and planning, investment, and governance on the other hand. While the family is discussing its vision, it also needs to consider the possible business scenarios that the management team is discussing – and explore how these possibilities will affect the family. It is critical for the family to have realistic expectations both of the business and of the demands that the business may make on them.

WHEN FAMILY BUSINESSES ARE BEST

- The family must explore and craft a unique vision based on their values, expectations, business potential and willingness to invest.
- The *Parallel Planning Process* supports planning for values and behaviors that support the concept of committed and capable ownership.

- Family commitment needs to be nurtured as the family grows and expands.
- The ultimate question that every business family needs to ask is about commitment: "Is the family willing to work together to perpetuate family ownership in this business?"

Part III

Strategies for the Family and Business

5 Family Strategy: Planning the Family's Participation

Family Actions

Business Actions

Five years ago the Wates Group was facing a dilemma. One of the UK's oldest and largest construction groups, it had been controlled by its founding family for more than a century. But now the five senior family leaders and owners were beginning to contemplate retirement. While several members of the next generation worked in the business, none had served in senior management or as directors – and there was uncertainty about who was interested in or capable of filling leadership and governance roles.[1]

The solution was not obvious, but one thing was certain: the Wates Group was not at all unusual. All family businesses face generational transitions – so planning for the family's development, participation, and succession is in effect planning for the business' continuity. Successful business families recognize the advantages of family participation in executive or governance roles – if there are sound structures and processes to ensure performance and to protect the family and business from conflicts. Planning to support the family's active involvement is a tangible demonstration to the next generation, the business, and its stakeholders of the family's commitment.

There is also a business interest in planning participation, and succession. Business families are an important source of employees, executives, directors, family leaders, and most importantly, owners. Developing family human capital is a competitive advantage of the family business model that cannot be replicated easily. Family businesses face many challenges but if the family plans well, developing the talent and commitment of its members, a special dimension is added to individual lives and the business legacy is strengthened.[2]

Planning for family education and development is powerful because it develops individual talent, making family members more capable and satisfied. The next generation's psychological needs are an important concern because growing up in a successful family is not easy. Consider the challenges facing a son or daughter in a famous family, and the expectations that are created by birth. These children often feel unworthy because they have done nothing to deserve the life they were born into. They can also feel powerless when they compare themselves to their successful parents and ancestors. Developing their talents and ensuring their contribution to the family's legacy is a life-enriching experience. Think for a moment what it would be like to be a young jazz musician if your father was Frank Sinatra.

THE SINATRA "FAMILY BUSINESS"

Franklin Sinatra Jr.'s story is a powerful lesson about the rewards of earning your place in the "family business" and why business families need to plan and support their next generation's development. Growing up in the Sinatra family, Frank Jr. was exposed to music at an early age. By his teens he was performing at local clubs, then he served a long apprenticeship with Duke Ellington, the jazz master. During his career Frank Jr. spent most of his time on the road performing in 47 US states and over 30 countries. He had guest appearances on several television shows and sang with his own band in Las Vegas as an opening act for bigger names. While he was well respected in the music business, just like his father, for his demanding rehearsals and setting high musical standards, he never achieved anything like the success of Frank Sr. But he never gave up, and in 1988 the father paid the son the ultimate compliment, asking him to serve as his musical director and conductor for his last series of live performances.

The Frank Sinatra Jr. story highlights the importance of preparation and participation in experiencing a meaningful life. Frank Jr. followed his father into the music business, completed an internship with a great teacher, worked outside the family business to gain experience, earned his father's professional approval, and contributed to the family legacy – not a bad accomplishment for anyone.

This chapter explores planning for the family's participation, development, and succession to a wide variety of roles. That planning, first and foremost, needs to promote the next generation's development so that family members become capable and satisfied adults, regardless of their participation in the business. Second, the family needs to ensure that proper agreements are in place so that members can actively participate without undue conflicts or difficulties. Third, family members need to be qualified so that they can contribute to the success of the business. Developing the family's potential, especially its leadership and ownership capabilities, is ultimately the family's responsibility – and no one else's.[3]

THE ADVANTAGES OF FAMILY PARTICIPATION

The family's relationship with the business endows them with influence beyond the number of shares they own. The Toyoda family (spelled differently than their company) owns a very small percentage of the shares in Toyota, the world's largest car maker, but the board of directors recently elected Akio Toyoda, the grandson of the founder, as president to lead the family business through a tough global recession. His family connection, combined with his strong experience in the auto industry, made him the ideal leader for the company his grandfather founded.

Serving as an ambassador for the company's ambitions and values makes a powerful statement in the marketplace. One of the new CEO's first assignments was driving with the Toyota racing team in the 24-hour Nürburgring endurance race – thus demonstrating Toyota's commitment to performance and engineering excellence.

Family participation may also serve in a tangible way to humanize the business by creating a brand with a "face," demonstrating the company's loyalty to employees, and strengthening customer and stakeholder relationships. Consider the way Jonathan Warburton, now chairman of the British family bakery, became the face of Warburtons through a television advertising campaign. In times of crisis family leadership and presence can even stabilize the entire organization. William Clay Ford, shortly after being named chairman in 1999, was one of the first executives on the scene when explosions badly damaged the Ford Motor Company's giant and historic River Rouge factory. His spontaneous comment that this was one of the saddest days ever for his family reassured the employees and the larger community that the Fords were with them, something that the most brilliant public relations staff could never replicate.

MANAGING GENERATIONAL TRANSITIONS

Generational transitions are a given for every family business because of the imperative of time. The senior generation leaders[4] must eventually step down and either sell the business or pass control to the next generation. Family business succession is a complicated interplay of senior and next-generation life cycles and the multiple transitions of roles and responsibilities. Succession planning in multi-generational

Figure 5.1 *The overlapping life cycles of two generations in a family business*

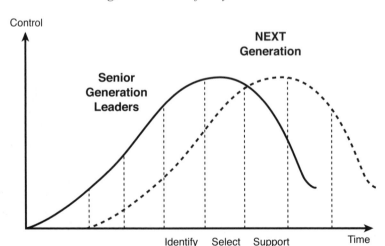

firms involves three key players: the head of the business, the chair of the board, and the chair of the family council.

Senior generation leaders plan and direct the succession process by identifying candidates, selecting a single successor or team, and in due course, supporting those appointed on the job (see Figure 5.1). Each of the succession phases creates the potential for review, adjustments, and delays because – even with the most careful planning – things can go wrong: deaths or other life events, underperforming successors, or business setbacks. It is tough for the older generation. Vasiliki Anyfioti, manager in William Grant & Sons and member of a Greek business family, describes her own experience: "They give you lots of opportunities, but at the same time they tend to undermine you, because they see you as a child."[5]

A family business that has not begun developing or implementing a succession plan is one that is not fully prepared to deal with the challenges of sustaining itself. The senior generation leadership is losing the opportunity to develop and test the next generation, and the next generation is missing out on the support and experience that the senior generation could have provided.

Even when there is a rigorous plan, the succession process is a challenge for any organization – and doubly so for a family firm. Harry Levinson of the Harvard Business School calls succession "a special problem of any [new] chief executive." He continues, "Whenever he or she changes something that his or her predecessor established or suggested, the very fact of making such a change becomes an indictment of the predecessor."[6] It is clear that in a family business, where the predecessor is a close relative, managing the transition requires especially careful thinking and planning. The backing of the predecessor is often critical to helping the successor establish credibility and support. The first time the new generation makes a change in strategy, the senior generation needs to be there to reassure the family and other stakeholders.

The planning and management of leadership and ownership transitions is an important test for the senior generation. Conflicting family, business, and personal issues often surface during the succession process. The priority is that the business needs capable leadership, but what if there are no strong family candidates? The selection of a non-family executive is a possibility but may upset the family. Tim Wates, fourth-generation owner and family leader, describes the positive impact on the family and business of a successful non-family CEO:

> I'm proud of how the business has done. It's transformed from being a good *family* business to an outstanding company. I'm proud that we've recruited excellent people and retained them. Our CEO is exceptional – one of the cleverest, most subtle people I know, and he's brought out the best in us. Most of all I'm proud that we've done this as a family.

Conversely, what if there are too many family candidates? The challenge of choosing one over the others, especially if the pool includes multiple sibling or cousin candidates, can also lead to family trauma. Musaab Al-Muhaidib, general manager of Muhaidib Technical Supplies, explains his family's solution:

> We have a charter signed by everyone above the age of 16. Everything is documented. It's essential because there are around 40 of us in the third generation. If we do things by the textbook, it's because we have to. The main criterion is competence. Whether the person concerned is a member of the family or not, we have the same requirements for anyone who works in the business. And we pay market salaries.

One very important issue is the conscious and unconscious motivations of senior-generation leaders in letting go of the reins.[7] They may not want to hand over the business after working their entire lives to achieve the control and accomplishment of leadership. There may even be feelings of regret at the sacrifices they have made in their family or personal lives, so the idea of stepping back is even harder to accept. In some cultures respect for the senior generation is such that its members always remain in charge. But, no matter what the family values or vision, planning for ownership and leadership succession needs the support of both generations.

Members of the senior generation have the power that comes with credibility, experience, family position, and ownership. So the succession process is difficult – if not impossible – without their involvement. If a senior family member chooses to resist planning or supporting the next generation transition, there is little that can be done. In the worst-case scenario seniors may choose to sabotage the process, and support successors whom they know to be incapable – but who present no challenge to their continued power. The case of the Steinbergs demonstrates a worst-case dilemma, which contributed to the failure of the business shortly after the founder's death.

"This is not the most qualified person we're selecting," Sam Steinberg explained to one of his non-family executives shortly after naming his son-in-law Mel Dobrin to succeed him as president of Steinberg Inc., at the time one of Canada's largest and most innovative retailers.[8] An accountant by training, Mel had joined the company on the grocery side and had climbed steadily upward through the corporate ranks. He knew the business inside and out and was a solid administrator.

Sam added, "It may be in the best interests of this corporation to have a professional manager. But I've had so much fun building and running this business that I wouldn't deprive my family of doing it." With this blunt admission, he confirmed what many already suspected. As long as Sam was around – indeed, for the foreseeable future – he would always lead Steinberg's, even though it was now a large public company responsible to thousands of shareholders.

For Sam, appointing Dobrin was the unattractive solution to an intractable problem. He was simply unprepared psychologically to surrender control of his company, so appointing his uninspiring and compliant son-in-law allowed him to maintain personal control. The appointment of Dobrin coincided with the beginning of a long, drifting decline at Steinberg's because of serious competitive threats and ongoing family conflicts. The business was declared bankrupt less than three years after Sam's death.

There are no magic bullets to overcome the senior generation's resistance to supporting the succession process but the planning ideas in this book help by allowing the entire family to develop a better picture of the current situation. It is easy for the senior generation to discount the next generation as not ready to lead the family business until they have proof otherwise. One of the benefits of the *Parallel Planning Process* is that working together provides an opportunity for the next generation not only to develop their skills but also to demonstrate their capabilities. When a family is planning together they share information and focus on action. The focus shifts from "When will the next generation be ready to lead?" to "How do we get the next generation ready to lead?"

Once a family agrees on a shared family business vision its members can begin working together to develop strategies that will address the

issues in question. The planning process also helps the senior generation to identify new behaviors beyond day-to-day management, created
by the growth of the family, which may not have existed previously (see
Table 5.1). It would be naïve to suggest that all founders and senior-
generation members can become enthusiastic about giving up their
central role in the family business, but it may be possible to help them
refocus some of their energies and consider new ways of participating.
Moving to building a family from building a business may seen like a
big move, but it can be more rewarding, and could support the senior
generation's need to give back and reconnect with the next generation
in a more supportive and nurturing way.

Some senior-generation members find it easier to step aside
completely in order to make space for the next generation. Mikhail
Kassam, a next-generation family member from Midas Safety in
Toronto, describes how his own father chose to exit the business:

> My father realized that the only way for him to manage the transition was to
> get out completely. We knew it wouldn't work if we were to be in the same
> office. After all, the opportunity to take over the day-to-day operations was
> a primary reason I decided to join the company full time.

After reducing their direct responsibilities, Donald and Doris Fisher,
founders of the Gap stores in the United States, spent time with their
grandchildren exposing them to the business and family philanthropy.
Donald would invite them to the business' headquarters for discussions
and lunch. Then Doris would talk to them about one of the family's
charitable activities. This is just one illustration of the possible ways
in which planning can help senior leaders, who fear their advice

Table 5.1 *Thinking about supporting senior
generation transitions to new family roles*

Business focused	Family focused
CEO role: executing	Chair role: mentoring
Living values	Transmitting values
Using power	Empowering
Business development	Family development
Business network	Family relationships

will no longer be sought, to contribute to the business and to create opportunities for expanded family participation.

The next generation will eventually lead and own the firm so, no matter what the succession process, a transition of ownership and leadership will occur. Social commentator Clive James, speaking on the BBC Radio 4 program *A Point of View* (December 25, 2009), used novelist Gabriel García Márquez's phrase for the twilight of a man's life – "the autumn of the patriarch" – to positively frame the senior generation's thinking about succession:

> There should be pride in it, that you behaved no worse. There should be gratitude that you were allowed to get this far. And above all there should be no bitterness. The opposite, in fact. The future is no less sweet because you won't be there. The children will be there, taking their turn on earth. In consideration of them, we should refrain from pessimism.

Professionalizing family and business roles

The first step in planning family participation and succession is to take a look at the family, business and ownership roles. Business roles are usually fairly well defined because they are based on management training and industry knowledge, and should entail position descriptions that spell out responsibilities and authority. Family and ownership roles are not so obvious, so the family needs to think about its vision and how to professionalize the family for leadership and ownership responsibilities. Shanti Poesposoetjipto, CEO of the family office and chair of the family's two operating companies in Indonesia shares her story: "My father planned to have five children, including two boys. He ended up with three girls. There was nothing said out loud about succeeding him, but looking back, he molded each of us to our potential. When he said he wanted a man to succeed him, I think he was preparing me for the real world."

A helpful tool for thinking about family business roles is Davis and Taguiri's model, which depicts a family business as three overlapping circles representing the different roles and perspectives of family, business and ownership (see Figure 5.2).[9] For example, any family member is usually concerned about his or her family's wellbeing. Give that person a job in the family business, and he or she starts thinking about compensation and promotions. Add ownership in the company and that family member becomes concerned about business performance and dividends. The three-circle model helps us think about what family members need to appreciate about the three roles in planning for family business participation.

Family

The family is at the center of our discussion as it provides the physical and psychological connections between its members. Family members experience psychological connection even if they are not employed by the firm and are not owners. This psychological ownership represents the individual's identity – growing up with the family business and being a part of the owning family. The simple act of carrying a famous business name exacts a price, and in a very real way creates a form of equity in the business. As the family's interests expand beyond the operating company to include other family enterprise activities, it is the family itself that presents individual members with the most opportunities for participation.

Family roles start informally and evolve over time, often reflecting the talents or influences of the individuals concerned. Historically the founder – traditionally also the father – has assumed the role of family leader and decision maker. At the same time, the mother has often

Figure 5.2 *Possible combinations of family business roles*

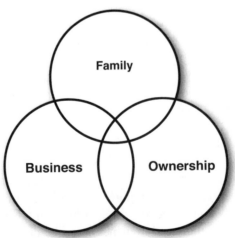

assumed the implicit and invaluable role of the family's other CEO, the Chief Emotional Officer. She works, usually quietly, at the critical tasks of family leadership. She interprets the behavior of one family member toward another, keeps communications open, makes sure that feelings are considered, promotes traditions, and plans special family functions. These arrangements can be effective, especially in first-generation entrepreneurial contexts, but by the second generation more formal planning is required to prevent overlapping responsibilities and possible conflicts.

Ownership

The ownership circle is usually populated by family members, but in some cases employees, private equity, or public shareholders may also be present. Typically, owners are concerned about making a good return on their investment from stock appreciation and dividends, but for family members the rewards can also include employment, prestige, family payouts, and other benefits. Ownership roles are usually connected to governance, such as membership or chairing of the board. Some business families will also develop a shareholders' assembly or owners' council.

Business

Family employees are significant stakeholders in the business because their careers and livelihoods depend on it. They also experience a closer and more regular relationship with the business than other family members. The primary concerns of family employees are interesting work, personal development, rewards and recognition, fairness, promotions, and job security. Employee, manager, and executive roles can become a serious source of conflict if the family has not developed clear agreements covering qualifications, promotion, and compensation. It is also important to have effective business governance to balance the management's decision-making power and to ensure accountability for behavior and performance.

However, one outcome of planning for participation and succession can be that the family agrees on descriptions for family and ownership roles with well-defined responsibilities and qualifications. A successful business and growing family may create many new roles and a continuum of activities in ownership and governance (see Figure 5.3). This figure could also be shown using the three circles because family members by definition hold multiple roles. The roles themselves are not as important as having a shared understanding of them among all family members – and applying it fairly. Even something as simple as the definition of a family member can require discussion. Some families define only blood relatives as family members, while others include in-laws.

The next step of planning for family participation is to identify activities that ensure family members have the right experience and education to be legitimate candidates for ownership and leadership roles.[10] This means putting education, training, and development processes into place. The family can always find roles for well-intentioned family members who want to contribute, but becoming a member of the board requires qualifications. Family board members need the skills and knowledge to work with professional managers and independent directors, or they become a roadblock to effective governance and create frustrations for all concerned. Daniel Echavarria, board member of Columbia-based Corona, and fourth-generation member of the business family, talks about the value of graduate business training to family board members:

> The beauty of the Master's in finance degree is that it helps you frame the issues and ask the right questions. The technical aspects of finance have been useful too. But the most important thing is that you need a Master's degree to become a member of the board (in our family)!

Encouraging family participation becomes more challenging as the family grows and multiple generations gain a stake in the business. Earlier generations usually find it easier to connect to the business since they typically have a closer link to the founder. They probably

Figure 5.3 *Possible family and business participation*

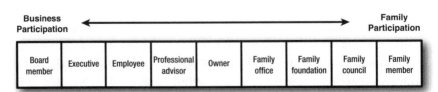

had an opportunity to learn about the business from the start and share the founder's early vision. Later generations tend to be motivated more by business performance, pride in the business, and their personal concerns. To prevent the older and younger groups splitting apart, the younger generation should be encouraged to learn about the family business, explore their possible involvement and consider the contribution they can make to the family's and the business' future success. The *Parallel Planning Process* supports this sharing of perspectives through the exploration of family values and vision. As we saw in Chapter 1, the Bancroft family could have had a very different outcome if the senior and next generations had spent time together talking about a shared vision for Dow Jones.

Preparing the next generation starts young

It is not an easy task to raise children who are truly interested in the family business, and – like most aspects of parenting – if we try too hard we can create resistance and even risk rejection.[11] Rolf Abdon, founder and CEO of Abdon Mills, is not really concerned about whether his children work in the family business:

> It is not a requirement that children be executives in the family business. Parents need to value the individual and future roles should reflect the child's interests. It is more important to support their happiness and respect their choices.

Every parent's first goal should be to help their children develop their special talents and interests. In many cases the family business can support this goal, but family business participation should be secondary to the child's personal development. The firm should simply be presented as a possible opportunity to have an interesting career and to support the family's legacy and values.

The next generation, however, may face its own demons about getting involved. Often children compare themselves with their parents or other family members, and find it difficult to believe that they could meet their family's expectations. They may also be anxious that any problems they had with their parents or siblings as they were growing up will be translated into problems in the business. Finally, there may be a strong fear of failure, compounded by the fact that a failure in a family business is shared with the entire family.

In more traditional cultures family obligations are higher priorities than individual needs. Vasiliki Anyfioti, an INSEAD MBA graduate already mentioned above, faced deciding between her family business and a consulting career as she approached her graduation in 1998. Her parents owned two businesses in Greece and Romania, and had supported her attending INSEAD to prepare their engineering-trained daughter for a general management role in one of the family firms. After many difficult discussions with her parents – and much soul searching – she chose not return to the family business, deciding instead to join a global consulting group. However, her career decision included delaying the start of her new job to spend six months helping her father through a difficult period of change, which involved professionalizing the management of one of his companies.

Ten years later, when guest lecturing to the family business course that she had taken herself, Vasiliki was asked by a student whether family obligation was a sufficient reason to join the family business. Her honest and heartfelt response captured her feelings about traditional families and family responsibilities. She was clear that her parents had never demanded that she return to the family business, but if they had, she would have felt strong pressure to accede to their wishes She went on to share that, since her parents had supported her both materially and emotionally, she felt she should reciprocate. Vasiliki currently serves as a director and informal advisor to her family business.

FAMILY OWNERSHIP ROLES

In the long run, ownership is what makes a family business a family business. As Ahmed Youssef, a family business consultant in Dubai, says, "true value creation by the family often lies in ownership and not management." Yet, unlike executive positions, the role of owner has no standard job description, training or qualifications. If the classified ad printed in Figure 5.4 were used for recruiting family business owners, who would apply?

Family members become owners through inheritance or gifting with full rights and responsibilities, no matter what their training, experi-

Figure 5.4 *Help wanted: family business owners*

Help Wanted: Family Business Owners

Significant responsibilities but no direct decision making authority. No written position description. No specific training or experience provided. No compensation, uncertain future goals, no support staff, and a lifetime commitment required.

The job requires– active participation and communication but no direct authority and success depends upon developing influential relationships with the senior generation, your siblings and cousins, and a board of directors.

Your actions will significantly impact your life, children's future, family's wealth, and family legacy for generations. The starting date is unknown and depends on the senior generation's wishes or unplanned events.

No need to apply: we will call you, maybe.

---

ence, or qualifications. Yet, despite the role's importance – indeed it is a key contributor to success in multi-generational family businesses – it is often poorly understood and neglected. In particular, the owners' authority and impact is often not fully appreciated. Owners elect the board of directors and therefore influence the selection of top management, the direction of the company, and even the company's continued existence. And, perhaps most significantly for the future character of the business, owners decide who will receive their stock, thereby creating the next ownership group. Adib Al Zamil, managing director finance and investment, Zamil Group, Saudi Arabia, makes a strong argument about preparing owners:

> One of our responsibilities is to have educated owners. It is not a question of employed or not. We need a culture where we (the family) make the right choices for the business. A family business is like a basketball team, all the players have to be prepared to contribute.

Planning ownership education

André Hoffmann, non-executive vice president of Roche Holding Ltd, suggests that family owners require a sound preparation to be most effective, including "a sound business sense, understanding how family businesses operate, being flexible in change, focusing on the long term and being willing to listen to others." Rolf Abdon, of Abdon Mills, expands on the need for qualified owners:

> Children in family business will inherit either the operating business or wealth, both of which require responsibilities. What is required is that they be responsible owners and support the management team through loyalty, engagement and proper motivation. Business owners need to be actively involved and knowledgeable about the business plan, how management executes the strategy, how to protect the family values and how to support the management team, especially if they are not in management themselves.

The challenges of ownership can be overcome only through education and experience. No one doubts the value of training and development activities for family executives. However, business families do not typically pay the same attention to ownership education. All too often, owners are not seen as important until a crisis or dispute requires them to become actively involved. Yet as a family business grows, so the role of the shareholders becomes increasingly significant to its long-term success.

This section addresses the specific knowledge and skills that owners should develop to be effective stewards for the family's business and wealth. Family owners need to understand six broad responsibilities:

- being business literate
- appreciating family values
- understanding the role of family ownership
- practicing stakeholder thinking
- learning about the business strategy and the firm
- appreciating governance and the role of the board and chair.

Business literacy

Developing a basic knowledge of the family firm can be especially challenging for those whose own career is not in business. Ownership education must be designed to inspire basic economic and business thinking as well as an understanding of the family business and how it operates. It must also encourage participation, particularly from the most inexperienced owners. In the first and second generation, family members are often steeped in the business' culture and absorb huge amounts of information about the firm, the industry, and business in general as if by osmosis. Over time, this connection weakens and the family needs to develop more formal methods of developing business literacy.

Family values

As we saw in Chapter 4, all business families have shared values that shape the firm's culture and dictate the way things are done. Future owners owe it to themselves and the company to understand the family values and business culture – first to protect what is of value, and second to influence change. Many next-generation owners, however, do not take the time to do this. They eagerly propose new ideas, seeking to introduce changes that reflect their personal identity, training, or experience. What these individuals must realize is that change in a family business is typically evolutionary – not revolutionary. A new culture will result from working on being successful with new practices and behaviors that built on the business' existing culture. This evolution should be a process of gradual movement based on the business' existing culture.

The first step to creating change in a family business is successfully working together before asking questions and having discussions about possible improvements. Family communication tends to work better when people appreciate the shared values that connect them, especially across generations. The traditional Chinese father and his Western-educated daughter will see management and the business very differently, but they still share the same core family values.

Ownership responsibilities

Shareholders concerned about the consequences of their actions and decisions need to understand their responsibilities. Being a capable and informed shareholder is about stewardship – protecting the business' future. The following questions provide a brief overview of what it means to be a capable owner:

- Do I have the business knowledge and understanding to analyze the performance of the firm and its management?
- Am I able and willing to participate in shareholder meetings and contribute to shareholder decision-making?

■ Do I understand my family's values and how the family's values influence the family and business?

■ What will be the long-term consequences of my decisions or actions on the family vision?

■ Do I consider the needs of all the stakeholders, including employees, the wider community, and other owners?

Stakeholder thinking

Owners need to understand how their actions and demands will affect other stakeholders in the family business. Traditional business thinking saw the business run for the benefit of the owners – with their interests placed above all others. Today, increasing shareholder value is no longer the only consideration – something that successful business families have always known. All stakeholders, especially employees and their communities, are affected by a business' actions – not just the shareholders. Family businesses have a competitive advantage if they build long-term and committed relationships with their employees, customers, suppliers, partners, banks, and the community at large.

Business strategy

As demonstrated throughout this book, planning is the recipe for business success. All companies have some type of plan – an implicit formula for creating a profit – even if it is not formalized. Future owners, partic-ularly those not employed by the family business, need to appreciate how strategic planning and investment can affect business performance. Understanding how decisions are made about the business and its strategy requires a working knowledge of the management's strategic planning processes (discussed in Chapter 6). It is also helpful to know about the firm's history, organization, and financial performance.

Yuelin Yang, senior executive in a Singapore shipping business, joined his Asian relatives in the family business after growing up in the United States:

> I practiced law for 9 years in Silicon Valley before coming to Asia at the age of 33 – knowing nothing about family business. My uncle was just looking for talent. At first it was a culture shock. Now I have a more balanced view. I can see that both the Silicon Valley business model and the Asian family business model have their merits. On the one side there's youth, speed,

creativity, and innovation. On the other there's tradition, conservatism, and relationships.

Appreciating governance

The board of directors is the structure that enables the ownership group to influence business planning and decision making. The *Parallel Planning Process* uses governance as a link between the family and business actions and performance. Family businesses require separate but interrelated governance structures for both the family and business. These are discussed in Chapters 8 and 9 respectively, but for now it is worth remembering that family governance is a much more complex topic than business governance because the structures and processes required depend on the family's values and commitment rather than statutes or legal requirements.

Planning next-generation executive development

Careers in the family business provide family members with a unique opportunity for personal growth and rewards – provided there is sound planning and clear family agreements. An attentive young family member will have spent his or her entire life learning about the family and business, so the first day on the job is preceded by many years of experience. A family member joining the business after completing years of education and outside work experience already has an insider's view, and starts with a significant advantage over a non-family member with the same qualifications and experience. There is also a higher degree of family trust that reduces concerns about confidentiality and motivation. This advantage, if well leveraged, enables the family member to take responsibility earlier and make a greater contribution to the firm than most non-family employees.

A well-conceived development plan for family executives gives the senior management team a realistic picture of each individual's career potential. The program should involve three activities: education (knowledge), training (skills and application of knowledge), and experience (performance). Together, these activities provide opportunities for members of the next generation to understand their own personal interests and future potential.

Such planning encourages high achievement and prepares the successor for leadership, thus smoothing the shift of power from one generation to the next. It can also provide personal motivation by helping the successor focus on long-term goals when faced with short-term challenges. As in a non-family firm, an effective executive career plan should:

- teach the knowledge and skills needed for a leadership role in the company
- support individual leadership style by progressively offering experience and responsibility
- develop a strategic vision of the firm instead of duplicating a view of the past
- provide personal insights based on mentoring, coaching, and performance assessment.

University or professional executive development programs are particularly important to family firms because family members tend to assume responsibilities at an early age and there is a mutual long-term interest in providing life-long development (see Table 5.2). Executive development plans will not always follow a smooth course. For some successors the sudden death, disability, or retirement of a parent rushes their development. Senior-generation family members may even be placed in situations where they need to resume an active role because of an unplanned event.

The family successor's career and development plan begins at home in the Growing Up phase and continues after retirement in the Senior Leader phase. Table 5.2 shows that after basic education and early experience in a business family the young person should have been exposed to business thinking and values. The Young Adult phase typically involves attending university, career exploration through internships, and gaining outside work experience to develop personal capabilities and self-confidence. Work experience outside the family business has advantages for the family, the business, and the individual. Family members should particularly consider working in another company immediately after university. Such experience provides them with an opportunity to test their skills and work with bosses who are not subject to family influences.

Table 5.2 *Family business career development time line*

Phase	Growing up	Young adult	Young professional	Manager/executive	Senior executive/director	Senior leader
Age range	0–18	18–30	25–35	30–45	35–65	55–75
Development activities	Family business exposure	Higher education	Functional experience	Executive and entrepreneurial experience: planning, decision-making and problem-solving	Leadership experience	Life planning; Exploring interests, talents, and activities
	Basic education	Internships	Graduate degree	Profit & Loss responsibility	Governance experience	Mentoring others
	Work habits	Career exploration	Mentoring	Executive education	Executive education	Transmitting values
		Outside life and work experience		Mentoring	Coaching	

Young Professionals join the family business full time in their mid-to-late twenties, and during the next five years or so they will gain functional expertise by working throughout the company, for example, in marketing, operations, and finance. In a Western or Asian family business they are then ready to take responsibility for a profit center in order to acquire general management skills. In the Middle Eastern context they are more likely to take on governance responsibility and to work with a managing director who has responsibility for the functioning of the business. Beyond this, young professionals may begin to explore outside resources such as a postgraduate degree or executive education to continue their professional development.

The Manager/Executive phase takes the successor through different learning experiences – and responsibilities he or she must understand to be a senior leader in the future. For example, he or she should lead a profit center, build a sales organization, or develop a new venture, preferably with profit-and-loss responsibilities and board review. This provides an appreciation of working with a board – and more importantly of rising to the challenges of investing, managing expenses, and making a profit.

Mentoring relationships help family employees learn valuable business principles, as well as how to manage people and time. Such teaching usually occurs over a period of a few years. After that, however, the mentor relationship tends to lose its effectiveness, because the protégé has developed new concerns or more senior responsibilities. When this occurs, it is important for the successor to develop a network of personal advisors or perhaps a coach.

The Senior Executive/Director phase is often the most personally challenging, as life events like death, divorce, and illness affect the family and the business. At the same time the firm's markets are probably maturing, and succession planning is becoming a pressing responsibility. One mistake that many families make is targeting their developmental activities at younger members. Unfortunately this fails to recognize that some people are active with the family business for their entire lives. In fact many become owners following the death of their parents – comparatively late in life. Executive education, coaches, and board members are thus important resources for senior executives and directors. Personal networks of trusted advisors, relatives, colleagues, or professional advisors can also be a source of social support and a sounding board for tough decisions.

The Senior Leader phase is about developing new personal interests beyond the business and sharing a lifetime of experience with the family and the firm in a constructive way. Becoming a mentor to either senior executives or directors – or perhaps high-potential younger family members – contributes to talent development. Senior leaders are in an ideal position to transmit values and support in non-business activities like philanthropy or a family office. Their credibility and the respect they have earned also give them a unique opportunity to support the family through tough decisions regarding strategy and ownership.

The most important long-term consideration in planning for talent development and career progression is continuous learning. As family members achieve senior executive roles and later become members or chair of the board, they will encounter new challenges in addition to the functional and general management skills they mastered earlier in their career.

FAMILY LEADERSHIP ROLES

As the number of family members and generations increases, the family requires more formal structures for planning and decision making. Tony Echavarria, former president of his family council and a third-generation member of a large Colombian family business, describes his experiences:

> You'd be surprised at how busy managing a family can keep you! It is prac-tically a full-time job for the chair of the Family Council. There are 60 of us now – all different ages in different places with different interests. This puts our governance structure under a lot of conceptual and logistic pressure, and needs constant management. There are no formal support staff, so it's just us, our printers, and our personal computers.

The nature of the formal structures will vary widely from one family to the next, but at a minimum there should be family meetings and some type of written family agreements (these topics are discussed fully in Chapter 9). Developing family leadership is just as important to the long-term health of the family business as finding a successor for the chief executive. The family leader cultivates family unity and sees that everyone feels appreciated in his or her individual roles. In smaller families the leader is likely to be a trusted family member, such as an older brother or sister working outside the business, or the spouse of the CEO. As more women become chief executives, the pool of applicants for the role of emotional leader is increasingly likely to include men. In larger families the chair and members of the family council often share aspects of the family leadership role.

Sometimes the various family leadership roles go unnoticed, but as the family matures and the business enters the Sibling Partnership or Cousin Collaboration phases, it is important that they are discussed as part of the family planning process. If the roles are explicit, everyone benefits – whether they work in the business or not – and there is a level playing field for access to information about the family and the business, which cuts down on tension and alienation. And keeping family members who are not working in the business involved may encourage them to contribute more in the future.

Jamie Crane, a senior family leader, speaking at a Kellogg Family Business Conference, offers some helpful insights about engaging the next generation:

> When we formed both the shareholders group and the family council we had fourth-generation members, typically college kids, go out with a third-generation person and interview different companies that had family councils. We had them travel to four or five different companies to see what they were like and what they were doing, and talk to the heads of their family councils. We really wanted the fourth generation to buy into what we were doing and understand it and be enthusiastic. So we had them form the family council. We had them present it to the family. I think it's very important that you involve the next generation.

THE WATES GROUP: DEVELOPING A NEXT-GENERATION LEADERSHIP STRATEGY

So what happened to the Wates Group, with which we began this chapter? How did the five senior leaders with no obvious family successors resolve their dilemma? As it turns out, the Wates provide a perfect example of the *Parallel Planning Process* in action. In their case, planning for the transition to the next generation of owners involved three steps. First, the family met, discussed their vision, and confirmed the importance of strengthening the management team with the best available talent. A decision was made to recruit an experienced non-family CEO from outside the business because that would support the generational transition process. With a new CEO and finance director in place, the family could turn its full attention to developing plans for its own transitions – of ownership and governance.

The second step was to engage an outside advisor to help prepare a comprehensive transition plan, focusing on developing the next generation's talents as professional owners and directors. A series of meetings helped the family confirm that, while they all believed in the business' future, several next-generation family members did not see themselves in leadership roles or even as owners. This prompted the family to assess its own talent pool objectively and to craft individual development plans for each of the committed next-generation members – using psychological assessments, coaching, executive education workshops, and governance experience. The results were successful. Two next-generation family members joined the Wates Group board, and two others became senior executives.

The final step of the transition was to restructure the ownership to reflect the decision by two members of the next generation to pursue careers and interests unrelated to the family business. A strong Wates family value was active ownership, so two senior family owners decided to request a buy-out of their branches after their children chose not to be involved.

The Wates family succeeded in their generational transition because they considered the linkage between family and business planning at each step. But the planning process was not over. The change in ownership, the next-generation leadership transition, and the appointment of a non-family CEO and chairman meant that the family needed a new family charter spelling out ownership roles and governance structures. As Andrew Wates, the former executive chairman of the group, says, "We are at the beginning of our family journey today, not the end of it."

In multi-generational family businesses there are several key roles that support the family's success. Leadership functions that were the responsibility of one or two family members in the early years now belong to a diverse family leadership team comprised of different interests, talents, and capabilities. As the family and business grow, the CEO's role must focus on the business' strategy and performance. This means that the family needs to take responsibility for ensuring that its members are prepared to serve on the family council, the board of directors, and the board's other groups, such as the family office or foundation. Clarifying and developing these roles and ensuring they are staffed with capable talent – family and non-family – are important outcomes of planning.

FAMILY PARTICIPATION AS A COMPETITIVE ADVANTAGE

The Wates case demonstrates the importance of planning for the next generation of family leaders – and of creating new roles as the family's relationship with the business changes. In addition to the new family charter, the Wates decided to create a new governance structure in the form of a family holdings board to ensure accountability and maintain family influence on the business. This new structure retains control of the family's financial investment and active participation in the core business as well as other family interests. Chaired by the former executive chairman and senior family member, it provides another forum for the family to share knowledge and support the development of the next generation. As the generations go by, the family's role increasingly becomes one of governance. Alignment of family and business governance processes among family, owners and management therefore becomes a vitally important family responsibility.

WHEN FAMILY BUSINESSES ARE BEST

- Family businesses face generational transitions that require planning to ensure the family is prepared for leadership and ownership transitions.
- Family participation is a competitive advantage if the family members are well trained and if there are sound structures and processes in place to ensure performance.
- The senior-generation leaders are the key actors in planning and ensuring next generation participation and succession.
- Business families must ensure ownership and leadership development. It is the family's most important – and often most neglected – responsibility.
- The ownership group needs to develop a sound understanding of business and finance concepts, an appreciation of the responsibilities of management, boards and shareholders, and an appreciation of the family business culture.

6 Business Strategy: Planning the Firm's Future

Family Actions

Business Actions

A few years ago "Anheuser-Busch acquires Interbrew" would have been the expected headline announcing the consolidation of the global beer industry. Anheuser-Busch, the world's most powerful brewer, was well positioned to lead an industry consolidation with its strong stock price, 50 percent share of the US market, and the industry's most recognized brand. So how did Interbrew (now InBev), a small European brewer operating in a country of 10 million people, become the industry leader and eventually acquire its much larger US competitor? There are no simple explanations for InBev's success, but there are useful lessons about the power of strategic thinking and business planning. The story provides an opportunity to compare how two family-led businesses did their planning – to create two very different futures.[1]

InBev's success partly reflects a superior business strategy driven by a creative management team and an ownership group committed to growing outside of Europe. They recognized early on that brewing would become a global business, that global scale mattered, and that – if they wanted to survive – they needed a new business strategy. Their analysis of their strengths, weaknesses, opportunities, and threats (SWOT) indicated that they were sound managers and marketers but that their growth opportunities were limited in Europe, a mature market compared with the Americas and Asia. InBev's response was a new global consolidation strategy to acquire other brewers in high-growth markets, to share management and governance roles, and to maintain strong controls especially on cost and quality. In contrast, Anheuser-Busch followed a legacy plan, protecting its U.S. domestic market, and developing only limited partnerships – just as it always had done.

Comparing these strategies clearly demonstrates how InBev was able to create a significant competitive advantage in terms of costs, marketing, and distribution. A sound business strategy sets the game plan and identifies the actions that translate the vision into new customers, a larger market share, and increased profits. In the case of InBev, a management team and board open to new ideas considered a wide range of opportunities beyond the firm's traditional geographic markets. We can also see how the two companies' different approaches towards planning family participation shaped their strategies. Management succession at Anheuser-Busch had seemed like a birthright for several generations, while naming an executive from an acquired company as CEO was simply unthinkable.

The most important lesson from this comparison is that business families need to think strategically about their legacy business strategy and focus on new opportunities. The question that In-Bev asked ten years ago was, "How do we leverage our strengths to grow globally?" InBev's executives, board, and owners answered that question, and acted by embarking on a global acquisition strategy. The result is that Anheuser-Busch is now a subsidiary of their firm.

Strategic planning is one of the most researched and studied management topics, so our intention is not to provide a comprehensive overview, but rather to explore strategic planning concepts in the context of parallel planning for family businesses.

UNDERSTANDING BUSINESS PLANNING

Planning is a critical activity for any organization, because it challenges the status quo by assessing the current situation, focuses attention on the future, and linking ownership and management goals. In simple terms business planning is making decisions about which customers to pursue, what products or services to sell, and where to invest the firm's resources – usually in people, technology, property, and equipment.

No matter how small or big, or simple or complex, all businesses engage in some type of business planning. There are three generic models. First, management can be *reactive*, adjusting to current events and taking decisions only about the immediate future. In small companies, when a customer orders a product, the manager orders more raw materials, schedules an employee to make it, and contacts the customer to ship the order. This is reactive planning.

As the business grows it typically uses the second model, *adaptive* planning, which looks at the wider environment of competition or changing market conditions. In this model management asks customers about future orders or checks out competitors to see what they are doing, then makes new plans for the business. If the customers report that they plan to buy 20 percent more of a new product during the upcoming year, management arranges to add new manufacturing capacity and have it ready to ship. If the competition adds a new product line or lowers prices to grow sales, management follows with similar actions. This model works with regional and medium-sized firms, where management has day-to-day control of the firm.

Once the firm grows in scale, complexity, or geography, it requires a *strategic* or long-term planning model based on identifying new opportunities for growth and exploring scenarios to exploit them. This third model of planning focuses decision making and action on the future. As Peter Drucker, the father of modern management, stated, "Long-range planning does not deal with future decisions, but with the future of present decisions."[2] Managers scan their environment for changes and trends and then position their companies in new markets based on the company's current capabilities – or new capabilities they are confident of acquiring. Large corporations need to think more strategically because their size requires them to coordinate actions and allocate resources accordingly. However, the other two models for planning can be equally effective – depending on the firm's size, complexity, market dynamics, and goals.

One weakness frequently seen in family businesses is a dependence on legacy strategies: repeating what has worked in the past rather than exploring new opportunities or directions. Theodore Levitt, in his *Harvard Business Review* article "Marketing myopia," captures this ethos:

Most managers manage for yesterday's conditions, because yesterday is where they got their experiences and had their successes. But management is about tomorrow, not yesterday. Tomorrow concerns what should be done, not what has been done. Should is determined by the external environment – what competitors (old, new and potential) can and might do, the choices this will give customers, the rules constantly being made by governments and other players, demographic changes, advances in generalized knowledge and technology, changing ecology and public sentiments, and the like.[3]

THE NEED FOR FAMILY BUSINESS PLANNING

As a family business grows or the founder–entrepreneur transfers responsibility and control to the next generation, the need for a strategic planning approach becomes clear. The planning processes for a family-owned business are similar to those of any comparable business of the same size – but with a longer time frame and greater concern for values and stakeholders. Closing a factory that the founder built in the family's hometown is not easy. The participation of family members in ownership, management, and governance also creates advantages and challenges that need to be addressed through planning.

Strategic family business planning can be driven by a wide range of goals:

- talent development: strengthening family and non-family human capital
- wealth creation: using family capital to earn positive returns
- entrepreneurship: developing new product or market opportunities
- social responsibility: making a contribution to communities or a nation
- family harmony: preventing family misunderstandings or conflicts
- reputation: maintaining a legacy based quality or service
- ownership continuity: building family commitment to encourage support
- reducing risk: protecting the family business' reputation and financial assets
- profitability: exploiting opportunities in the external environment.

This chapter looks primarily at *business* planning, but places it in the wider context of other family activities. Business families need to think strategically at two levels: first, that of the operating business or businesses; and second, of the family's other assets or activities, including the new ventures, investments, and philanthropic endeavors. These two levels of planning require coordination because the operating businesses often supply the resources to fund or support the family's other activities. It is also important to think about the operating businesses as part of a diversified portfolio of financial investments designed to manage risk. Sam Johnson, the former chair of Johnson Family Companies, used strategic planning in the operating companies as a tool to reduce risks to the family arising from competition, government regulation, and taxes. As he stated in a Kellogg case study, *Succession and Continuity for Johnson Family Enterprises*, "For a family business, diversifying is a hedge against risk. If we have pockets of entrepreneurship, we have more than one shot at being in business 100 years from now."

The strategic planning model presented here is rigorous and includes governance thinking, which many strategic planning models neglect. It is designed to help owners, junior family members, and non-executives appreciate strategy concepts. It is also useful to senior executives and board members as a tool to rationalize strategic processes or to communicate about them in a less technical manner. We will introduce the model through the story of one family shareholder, as she learns how her financial investment and the business strategy work together to create economic and social value.

What every family member needs to know about strategy

Sally is not employed by her family's business but she is an important shareholder and feels connected to the business that her grandfather founded and her uncle currently leads. Her training and work as a lawyer mean that she understands business matters, and she tries to keep up with developments in the family firm. However, like many family business shareholders her only real contact is through the dividend she receives twice a year. After reading the most recent online shareholder update, she was concerned that the management was thinking about changing its strategic direction, borrowing more money, and reducing the annual dividend for the first time in ten years.

She immediately called up the chair of the board, who is also her aunt. After a few pleasantries she asked, "What is going on here?" Her aunt told her that the company was faced with competitive threats that would require a period of increased investment. Sally was uncomfortable with this explanation. The business had long benefited her and her family – and she took great pride in the company that her father served for many years as vice president and board member right up until his death. On the one hand she did not like the sound of the changes and was not sure why they were necessary. On the other hand she wanted to be a supportive owner – but did not know how to begin assessing the management's recommendations to the board. Sally wants to understand the threats facing her firm more clearly, and the long-term benefit that the increased investment will generate for all stakeholders.

Like Sally, all family shareholders first need a basic understanding of strategy. Usually, their share of the family business is their largest investment, and they need to know how strategic decisions will affect their position – including risk, dividends and return on investment. Like many family owners, Sally feels a sense of psychological ownership, but in times of change, understanding strategy is essential to sustaining this emotional stake in the business. Management also functions better and can make more effective decisions when it feels it has the commitment of the owners. For all these reasons, learning the basic principles of strategic planning is essential to shareholders like Sally and her family business.

Businesses face constant change. Markets evolve and innovative competitors are always fighting for greater market share. To stay competitive, businesses must continuously improve and reinvest. Identifying where to compete and the type of investment are the fundamental strategic decisions made by any business. And assessing the opportunities and threats of the industry in relationship to the firm's strengths and weaknesses largely makes that decision. These factors determine the level of investment necessary to exploit new opportunities and protect the firm's competitive position in its industry.

The strategic planning process thus looks at trends in market share, and the financial and organizational resources of the company. The assessment of the firm's strengths, weaknesses, opportunities, and threats is called a SWOT analysis. It also aims to articulate the company's core competencies (what it does well) and its competitive advantage (what it does better than the competition). This analysis seeks to document the potential of the business to create economic value for its shareholders and stakeholders.

The second stage of the planning is about how resources should be targeted to sustain or increase the company's competitive advantage. At this stage, different strategic priorities and directions are discussed and a number of basic business strategies are reviewed. In family companies, the impact of different strategies on family ownership also needs to be assessed. As we have seen in previous chapters, a family business strategy can only work if it is consistent with the family's values and vision of ownership – and that includes expectations for return on investment and distribution of dividends.

After these assessments are complete, several scenarios are developed and analyzed by the management and the board. From these alternatives, a final strategy is chosen and an investment decision is made. The roles in this process are clear. Sally's uncle, the CEO, and his management team drive the strategic planning process, while the board of directors, chaired by her aunt, serves to ensure that the management's strategies reflect the best interests of the shareholders and company and will maximize value creation within the owner's tolerance for risk. However, the board also serves the vital function of challenging the management's assumptions and of providing an objective review of the proposed strategy. Shareholders seldom have a direct input in developing the strategy, but their values, vision, and shareholder value proposition should be a part of management's strategic thinking (see Chapter 4 for a discussion of shareholder value proposition). In family companies, the board or family council fulfills the vital role of ensuring the proper alignment of business strategy and ownership expectations.

All businesses and their markets mature over time, resulting in different competitive and economic situations and a changing need for reinvestment. Similarly, as businesses age and grow, their strategic potential changes. In family businesses, ownership also goes through life cycles. With time, ownership becomes increasingly dispersed, and – as we have seen in previous chapters – the investment objectives of shareholders often change. Strategically aligning business and ownership objectives thus becomes more challenging – and critical.

Family shareholders like Sally need to understand how the natural life cycles of their business or its industry will have an impact on the levels of reinvestment needed. The family business advantage depends on balancing the trade-off between strategic investment for the future and shareholder pay-outs in the present. Privately held family companies tend to grow capital internally, through retained earnings. As the proportion of earnings paid out to shareholders increases, the rate of internal capital growth decreases, leading to lower levels of strategic reinvestment. However, because of their close relationship with shareholders, family businesses can adjust their capital growth rates over time to match their firm's strategic need.

All businesses have limited capital to deploy. Publicly listed companies compete for capital – and the cost of that capital can vary considerably over time. Industries fall in and out of favor with investors, and markets move up and down. Privately held businesses with owners like Sally typically have lower, more stable costs of capital, which can give them a significant advantage over other companies. This "patience" of family capital may even explain why family firms perform well. Their close-knit ownership groups are more willing to adjust their reinvestment levels for the long-term strategic benefit of their businesses. This is particularly true when the family owners are actively engaged with the business.

In short, family owners like Sally need to know the "strategic story" of their business, including the potential for growth in their market and the life cycle stage of their business. They should learn the basics of their industry, as well as understanding the core competencies and underlying values that have historically contributed to the success of the business. They should know about the general organizational structure of the company, its governance, and how roles and responsibilities are defined. They should know the current competitive goals of the company and the business strategy for accomplishing these goals in the future. Even if they are not on the board, they should be able to question the management's assumptions and provide rigorous, independent assessment of any recommended strategies.

In family businesses, profit and reinvestment are usually mutually dependent and grow in tandem. Family owners should not only track growth in net income, but should also know how efficiently their business produces profits. Another factor that drives long-term value creation – arguably the most important of all – is the ability to change. Businesses that stay the same eventually fall behind. Family owners should be aware of key strategic innovations and why they are being undertaken.

However, understanding strategic planning can be challenging for family owners like Sally. As businesses and their owning families grow larger, generating mutually beneficial strategic thinking takes careful planning and a shared process. When owners like Sally know what it will take to create long-term value, they tend to support reinvestment at appropriate levels, giving their companies a family business advantage. Following, then, is a simplified guide to strategic planning. We created it with Sally in mind, but it is designed to be of use to anyone involved with family business.

DEVELOPING STRATEGIC PLANS FOR FAMILY BUSINESSES

Strategic planning for any operating company is about assessing the firm's capabilities and matching those capabilities with market opportunities to create value.[4] This is also at the heart of the *Parallel Planning Process*. Traditionally family businesses have relied on legacy strategies or replicating past successes. This practice – built on the assumption that change is incremental – worked well until the late twentieth century, which heralded a global business environment of turbulence, threats, and unimaginable opportunities. This dynamic environment reduces the value of adaptive planning, and requires a more entrepreneurial approach based on scanning the horizon for new opportunity, sharing risk through partnership, and rewarding innovation and value creation.

Strategic planning always creates a dynamic tension between different stakeholders with different perspectives and goals. The CEO and management team see the process as their opportunity to shape the firm and its future, the board members want to ensure they are protecting the firm's continuity, the owners – whether or not they are closely involved – have their own expectations, and other stakeholders want their specific concerns addressed. Consequently it is the CEO and management who must engage the other parties and ensure that they are a part of the process and understand the planning agenda.

Developing a business strategy is a process, not an event or annual ceremony. It does not happen in a two-day meeting held offsite and attended by the board and key executives. It needs to be a part of the firm's way of working together, integrating business development, performance assessment, opportunity recognition, and the owners' expectations and vision. These events should be part of an ongoing strategic thinking process (see Figure 6.1). Some boards participate by dedicating time at each of their meetings to exploring parts of the firm's business model and inviting key executives to share their perspectives. Some firms have strategic planning task forces that meet throughout the year to provide updates on different issues. This approach makes strategy development a tool for better communication and stronger engagement, which not only encourages broad ownership of the strategy but also makes it a vital part of daily activities.

There are four interrelated steps to the strategic planning process: Strategic Thinking, Strategic Direction, Action Planning, and Oversight. We will explore the first two in depth because they are the foundation of the business planning process that is so important to this book. The third is about implementing strategy, this is execution and could form another entire book, so we will not discuss it here, while the fourth is governance addressed in Chapters 8 and 9.

The first step, Strategic Thinking, involves engaging the stakeholders and collecting information about the firm, the owners' expectations, potential opportunities, and risks. The desired outcome is an agreement on the firm's potential for value creation based on analysis of the information collected and different assumptions that are used to craft possible strategic scenarios.

Ultimately, strategy is about the firm engaging with its environment. The second step is therefore the decision by management and the board on a strategic direction for the firm. The Strategic Direction is the master plan that shapes all of the firm's activities. Six generic types of strategic direction are discussed later in this chapter.

Once the Strategic Direction has been agreed, the Action Planning step leads to implementing the strategy. This is fundamentally the management of the business and its activities. Executives and staff develop timetables for action, monitor performance, and coach for results. Managers also review the ongoing implementation and reformulate tactics as needed.

The final step that links all the activities together, crafting accountability and feedback for the entire planning process, is Oversight. While the CEO drives strategy development and implementation, the board reviews the plan, monitors performance against the plan, and ensures

Figure 6.1 *Business strategy for operating units*

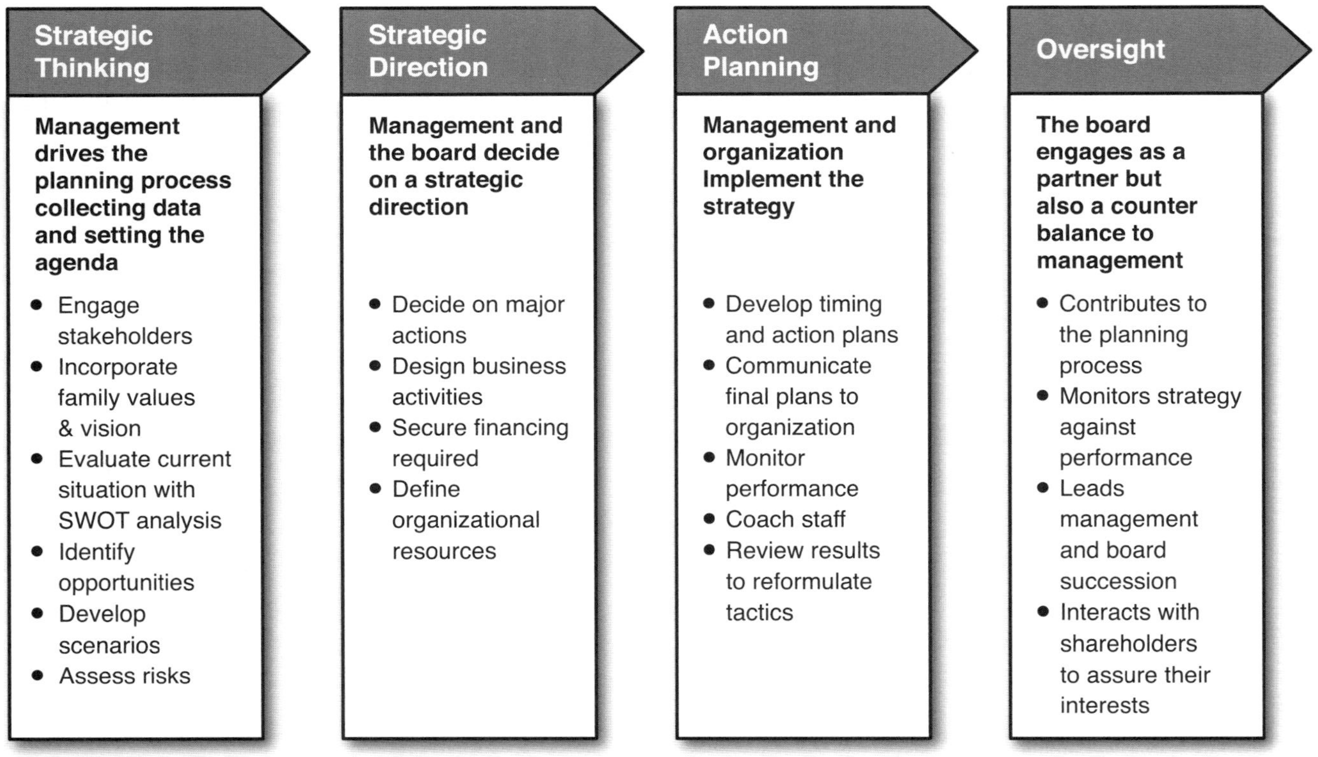

Strategic Thinking	Strategic Direction	Action Planning	Oversight
Management drives the planning process collecting data and setting the agenda	**Management and the board decide on a strategic direction**	**Management and organization Implement the strategy**	**The board engages as a partner but also a counter balance to management**
• Engage stakeholders • Incorporate family values & vision • Evaluate current situation with SWOT analysis • Identify opportunities • Develop scenarios • Assess risks	• Decide on major actions • Design business activities • Secure financing required • Define organizational resources	• Develop timing and action plans • Communicate final plans to organization • Monitor performance • Coach staff • Review results to reformulate tactics	• Contributes to the planning process • Monitors strategy against performance • Leads management and board succession • Interacts with shareholders to assure their interests

accountability. These steps are reviewed in detail along with planning tools to support the creation of the strategy plan.

Beginning the Strategic Planning process: Assessing the business and its current situation

Businesses stay competitive by continuously assessing their strengths, weaknesses, opportunities, and threats to support strategic planning. This is not at all the same thing as continuously monitoring sales and financial results. Planning is about analyzing a company's situation beyond its operating results to understand the underlying factors and competencies that it can use to build a competitive advantage.

The SWOT analysis (of strengths, weaknesses, opportunities, and threats) mentioned earlier is where management generally starts thinking about the company's current situation and generating new ideas about the future (see Figure 6.2). Internal assessment explores the firm's capabilities (strengths and weaknesses) related to assets,

Figure 6.2 *The SWOT analysis of the organizational strengths and weaknesses and the environmental opportunities and threats*

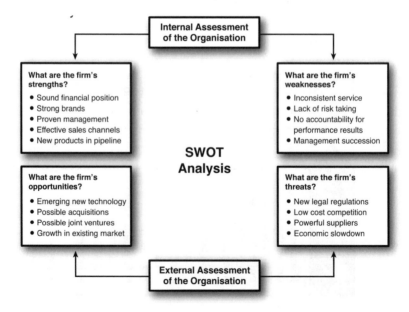

resources, technologies, and skills. Usually, management examine the particular strategic capabilities in finance, marketing, and organization to assess their potential contribution to any strategic plans that may be proposed. What the firm does better than competitors or in a unique way will generally be the basis for creating a new strategy. For example, a company with a sophisticated distribution system may want to identify related or new products for a diversification strategy in order to capitalize on its distribution skills.

Strategic thinking about the firm's future potential

The SWOT analysis provides management with information on the firm's current position and future potential. This information is analyzed using a two-dimensional matrix that plots the strength of the firm's capabilities and the attractiveness of its external environment to create a measure of the firm's Strategic Potential. The Strength of the Firm's Capabilities reflects resources, such as leadership talent, finance, brands, technology, and distribution, which could all represent a competitive advantage. The Attractiveness of the External Environment is defined as the desirability of the firm's market based on economic and competitive factors, such as growth rate, competitive pressures, government regulations, taxes, change, profitability, and new opportunities.[5]

The model (see Figure 6.3) shows Strategic Potential based on nine possible combinations of the two variables. The three boxes labeled A represent high to medium market attractiveness and high to medium capabilities. The boxes labeled B represent a mix of market attractiveness with firm capabilities (low market attractiveness with high firm capabilities or a medium score on both variables). The boxes labeled C represent low on both dimensions-or a combination of low and medium.

The Strategic Potential Model assumes that firms competing in attractive markets and with strong internal capabilities have better potential to create value for their shareholders. Attractive markets are more conducive to higher growth and better profitability, while capable organizations are associated with the ability to exploit whatever strengths they have as competitive advantages. Warren E. Buffett, the investment guru, identifies these two variables of strategic potential as

Figure 6.3 *Strategic potential model of business value creation*

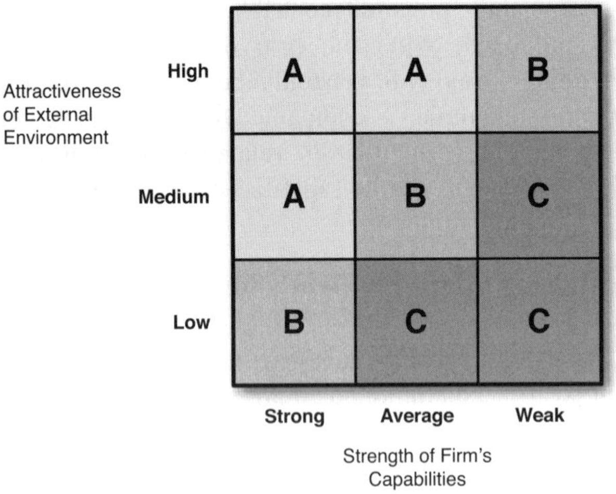

ideas that shape his investment thinking. Speaking to the *Wall Street Journal* on December 10, 2009, he reiterated his philosophy about the importance of an attractive market with his often stated quote: "When a management with a reputation for brilliance tackles a business with a reputation for bad economics, it is the reputation of the business that remains intact." On the importance of a capable organization, meaning good leadership, he also sounds a clear warning: "You should invest in a business that even a fool can run, because someday a fool will."

Determining the business' Strategic Direction

We use the firm's Strategic Potential (based on an assessment of its current position and its future potential) for evaluating possible business strategies and considering investment options. The attractiveness of the environment and the firm's capabilities are limiting factors in selecting the firm's strategic direction. A firm in the three upper-left-hand boxes labeled A in Figure 6.3 is a strong business in an attractive environment, and can pursue Market Leadership or Expansion strategies that are not available to firms in the boxes labeled C. The latter are relatively weak businesses in unattractive environments. These firms face the most serious threats because they lack both a positive market situation and the strengths to exploit a new opportunity.

However, many family firms fall into the middle ranges, labeled B. These businesses are moderately successful but have greater potential if management can identify new opportunities. A SWOT analysis often reveals that they have weaknesses in their business capabilities or are in unattractive markets. The Wates Group, already encountered in the previous chapter, made a difficult decision to exit their traditional business of house building based on an assessment of their strengths and opportunities. Tim Wates, fourth-generation owner and family leader, says:

> We made a difficult decision to exit our heritage business, which is house building, a few years ago. Today we're a big contractor and 80 percent of our work is for the public sector, so we haven't noticed the downturn. Our philosophy is that we shouldn't do something unless we think we can be brilliant at it. We're not completely brilliant yet, but we're getting there!

The goal of business planning is to position the firm in an attractive market where its strengths create a competitive advantage. This means moving the business toward the A positions (see Figure 6.4). Strengthening the firm's strategy means identifying actions that will enable the firm to make this move. Determining a family firm's Business Value Creation

Figure 6.4 *Strengthening the firm's strategic position*

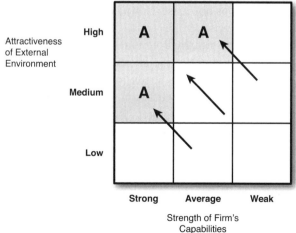

Potential is a valuable activity for owners and managers to undertake together because it builds a shared awareness of the firm's situation. This exercise naturally leads to thinking about the type of strategy the firm needs to pursue. A strong firm in a growing market is probably not going to abandon its position, whereas most people would understand that a weak firm in a declining market needs to make some changes.

Strategic Direction and tactics for Action Planning

By this point in the planning process, management should have gained many insights into their company's current situation and possible new business opportunities. The internal and external assessments should have provided management with a solid understanding of the firm's Strategic Potential – based on the firm's internal capabilities and the nature of the external environment. The next challenge facing management is to determine the firm's Strategic Direction and alternatives based on the firm's Strategic Potential. These strategy alternatives provide the input for the final decision on a business strategy and the family's investment commitment (discussed in Chapter 7).

The process of determining a Strategic Direction challenges the organization's thinking on what decisions and actions need to be taken in order to improve or strengthen its position. Fundamentally, there are six basic possibilities: market leadership; market expansion; redeploying assets in new opportunities; entrepreneurship; strengthening capabilities; and, last but not least, exiting altogether. Each is covered in more detail below.

The discussion about Strategic Potential should leave no doubts about the management's assessment of the current situation and which of the six Strategic Directions the firm needs to consider. Take the case of two electronics manufacturers in different industries. One is the eighth largest competitor in a mature market; the other is the eighth largest competitor in a high-growth market. These two companies could be similar in size, financial structure, and organizational skills, but they face very different challenges for growth and creating a competitive advantage.

After reaching agreement on the firm's current situation, possible opportunities and the attractiveness of different markets the management team needs to begin their detailed discussions about Strategic Direction. Remember, the Strategic Direction represents the firm's approach to deploying its resources and engaging with its environment to strengthen its competitive position and capture market share. These discussions are driven by three generic questions:

- How should we respond to changing conditions, new opportunities and threats?
- How should we allocate resources and capabilities?
- How should we compete to create customers?

Figure 6.5 overlays the six Strategic Directions with the Strategic Potential Model to identify which might be most appropriate, given management's assessment of the industry and the firm.

Using the Strategic Potential matrix as a template the six directions are positioned to show how they relate to the firm's capabilities and the external environment. For example, a firm with a strong Strategic Potential based on strong capabilities and an attractive market would consider Strategic Directions such as Market Leadership or Market Expansion. A firm in the lower right quadrant with weak capabilities and low external environmental attractiveness would consider Exit strategies to protect the family's capital.

Figure 6.5 *How Strategic Potential influences Strategic Direction*

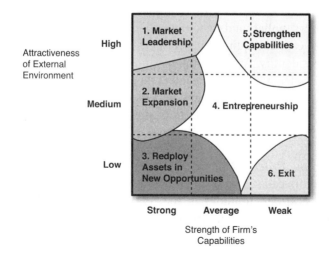

It is important to note that the Entrepreneurship option is always available as a Strategic Direction. Entrepreneurial strategies are a tool for innovation such as creating a new market or changing an existing market. Amazon and Apple are examples of firms that used an Entrepreneurial strategy to create their market positions, and are now using a Market Leadership strategy to consolidate these new markets. These strategies may not always be within the limits of the firm's Strategic Potential, but risk-taking managers pursue them anyway.

Figure 6.5 also shows an Exit strategy and the all-too-common reality that, if the firm's owners are reluctant to invest or have refused to take strategic action to strengthen the firm's position, the business should be sold. Sometimes in such cases, a generational transition of management and ownership can Redeploy Assets in New Opportunities or use Entrepreneurship as a basis for regeneration of the business. There follows a detailed description of these and the other possible Strategic Directions.

Market Leadership

This is the most aggressive strategic approach, intended for firms which can fully exploit their strengths in their existing attractive markets. Market leaders capitalize on their advantages by aggressively investing more money in new products, capturing market share and accelerating growth. They build barriers of entry to discourage potential competitors from realizing profitable opportunities in the market. Such barriers may include threats of lawsuits over patent infringements, long-term contracts with suppliers and customers, changes in product specifications that increase capital requirements for new entrants, or the creation of a strong brand identity. Apple Computer, now just Apple, is an example of Market Leadership. It has expanded its product line from computers to MP3 players to phones and now tablets, using music downloads and software applications to build barriers and expand globally. Examples of specific tactics include the following:

- *Expand the Product Offering.* Broaden coverage of niches so that competitors can see no unfilled opportunities that could ultimately lead to a strong foothold in the market. Offer a wide range of products and services in order to take full advantage of business strengths.

- *Consolidate the Industry.* Acquire competitors to strengthen market position and increase operating efficiencies. Successful acquisitions may leverage brands, core competencies or technology – resulting in increased profitability.
- *Expand Globally.* International expansion can take many forms and is available to firms of all sizes because of improved communication and transport links. Today national firms are using their market leadership experience in one country as a basis for an international market leadership positions. Starbucks, Louis Vuitton, and Sony are examples of global market leaders.

Market Expansion

This is closely related to Market Leadership and suits a firm with strong capabilities but a less attractive market. These capabilities allow it to compete at a high level, but the less desirable market limits the potential returns. Volkswagen represents a Market Expansion approach. The automobile industry is struggling but Volkswagen's goal is to be the top performer in the global market. It has many existing strengths, and the management has come up with many new ideas to improve the company significantly. Examples of specific tactics include the following:

- *Expand into New Market Segments or Geography.* Take the great strengths of the business and pursue new types of customers based on current usage, new products, new distribution channels, or entirely new customer demographics. Geographic expansion requires moving from a local to a regional or regional to national operation. This is a logical progression for a well-managed company with strong management and control systems.
- *Integrate Forward.* Expand by moving downstream in the product flow, enter customers' markets by acquiring some of them – or go into competition with them. Note, however, that this is among the riskiest of all Strategic Directions, as it puts the company in new markets that existing managers may not understand. The advantages include making savings, gaining full control of the product and opportunities for Innovation. This strategy also runs the risk of offending and losing current customers who might resent doing business with a supplier who is also a competitor. In short, this strategy requires tremendous business strength.

■ *Integrate Backward*. Add increased profitability to the current business by improving access to raw materials or products at an earlier stage of the supply chain – such as making what the company used to buy. Assemble in-house what was once outsourced, paint what was delivered fully painted, package what was packaged elsewhere, and so on. Like forward integration, backward integration can be accomplished through acquisition of another company or through internal development. But it is typically a less risky path than forward integration.

Redeploy Assets in New Opportunities

Do this if the business is strong, but the market and industry are mediocre. This frequently occurs when a family firm stays in a maturing industry too long, or fails to invest in new opportunities. Such an assessment should prompt managers to harvest assets and redeploy the financial resources in a stronger market. That is, they should extract funds from the company in order to spend them elsewhere on new opportunities. The Dayton family, owners of the Dayton-Hudson Department Store Group (Target, Dayton's, Hudson's, and Marshal Field), used a redeployment strategy of low-growth businesses to fund the expansion of their Target discount stores, a potentially high-growth area. Examples of specific tactics include the following:

■ *Exploit Fastest-Growing Market Segments*. Even mature markets, such as manufacturing or retailing, boast pockets of high growth ranging from new distribution channels to e-commerce. A strong company can identify these segments and decide to enter them aggressively.
■ *Harvest Products or Markets*. Eliminate mature products and/or marginal customers. Perhaps planning reveals a need to maximize the return from the current business in order to redeploy funds into new, more attractive markets or business opportunities. Companies may harvest some income by selectively raising prices to discourage less profitable customers. Companies might also choose to discontinue less profitable mature products.
■ *Stop Reinvesting*. Planning may reveal that the business is stronger than the future of the market warrants. If the company is a high-quality operation, it might consider becoming only average in its

product or service quality. If it is a low-cost supplier, it might cease to emphasize that advantage and allow the cost of operations to rise slowly. It could then funnel the freed cash into new market opportunities.

■ *Increase Profit Margins*. Harvest cash from a deteriorating market by raising prices or cutting expenses on all products and services. Again, the purpose is to funnel the cash into a fresh business.

■ *Diversify into Related Markets*. This strategy applies a company's current strengths to new but related markets. For example, a bicycle manufacturer might begin making stationary exercise equipment, perhaps with the same brand identity or distribution system. A seafood distributor might add a line of sushi products. Market weaknesses require the business to identify new opportunities where it can effectively use its strengths.

■ *Focus on New Applications*. Another approach for a business facing weak Strategic Potential is to find new uses for old products that do not need much adapting. For example, a firm that sells thermostats can explore new niches in the sustainable energy market.

■ *Diversify into New Businesses*. Although the business itself may be fairly strong, related market opportunities may be unattractive. Funds may be better spent on new types of businesses. An industrial products manufacturer might move into manufacturing consumer products, or a restaurant might develop a line of frozen foods.

Entrepreneurship

This represents a large part of the center of Figure 6.5 because it is often the strategic position occupied by family businesses. In some cases the business may be performing at an acceptable level but in an unattractive market. In others the market may have deteriorated and the family business has continued with lower profitability and reduced investment. Either way the organization needs additional capabilities. These could be new capital, a replacement for legacy strategies, new management skills, or stronger governance.

Firms with medium environments and average capabilities are good candidates for Entrepreneurship strategies led by the next generation. After all, the business currently offers limited growth in shareholder value creation and will not be able to support the next generation without some kind of innovation based on a new vision of the firm and its market. Typically an Entrepreneurship strategy means investing in new technology or partnerships unrelated to the firm's past experience. One of the best examples of family entrepreneurship is Louis Vuitton Möet Hennessy, the luxury products group, which has acquired or created companies in wine and spirits, jewelry, perfumes and cosmetics, fashion, and retailing in a wide range of industries. Examples of specific tactics include the following:

- *Identify Totally New Opportunities*. An entrepreneur who identified a market opportunity and created a product or service is the origin of most family businesses. But this type of innovative strategy can also help a small or weaker company increase its profitability several generations down the line.
- *Create a New Partnership, Joint Venture, or Strategic Alliance*. This can include licensing, franchising, joint marketing agreements, overseas manufacturing, and importing or exporting. Alliances can be forged with suppliers, competitors, buying groups, customers, or any other organization that can create and support value creation.
- *Change Industry Practices*. Pursue strategies that keep competitors off-balance by rewriting the rules of the game. This might be a matter of altering the industry's seasonal pattern of promotional expenditures, selling through a new channel, offering new credit terms, or providing a new package of related services such as training or support programs.
- *Adopt New Technologies*. Here, industry and environmental analysis will have revealed emerging technologies that create opportunities for a new direction.
- *Seek Market Niches*. If a company's weaknesses do not allow it to compete effectively in the larger market, management might identify a few niches (such as local deliveries, private-label production, or a particular group of customers) that they can target. These may not be big enough for larger, stronger competitors, or they may be too demanding for them. As a result the business will operate in a relatively sheltered environment, which may help it gain sufficient strength to broaden strategy later on.
- *Improve Operating Effectiveness*. In situations where neither the market nor the business promises exciting new directions, correcting internal weaknesses often becomes the core of future strategy. Such

opportunities, revealed through the planning process, might include offering a higher level of service or customizing products.

Strengthen Capabilities

This should be done if your firm lacks the business capabilities to compete despite having good markets. The focus of this Strategic Direction is developing an organization capable of supporting a more effective business strategy. The weak competitive condition of the business requires innovative ideas to take advantage of attractive industry and market circumstances. Examples of specific tactics include the following:

- *Improve Competitive Advantage.* Take the firm's strengths and enhance them. If customers perceive the business as a quality supplier, invest money in strengthening those perceptions. If the firm has the advantage of being a lower-cost supplier, strengthen that reputation.
- *Overcome Competitive Disadvantage.* If, for some reason, customers do not prefer the company's product or service, identify the chief relative disadvantages – a weak sales force, an inferior product, a high price – and work to rectify them.
- *Acquire New Business Skills.* Purchase a firm that is strong where your company is weak – one that has more plant capacity perhaps or a larger, more effective sales organization. Or recruit and hire people with the specialized skills necessary to strengthen the business. For example, an international opportunity may justify the investment in staff with global marketing competencies. When it is too late for the company to build up the necessary skills internally, acquiring them is the only alternative.
- *Copy the Competition.* When a company's market and business strength do not justify speculative investment and competitors are obviously pursuing superior ideas, the best strategy may simply be to mimic their products, use similar packaging, provide the same kinds of services or replicate their pricing and promotion methods.

Exit

The very weak business in a very weak environment usually has only one option. The owners must divest themselves promptly before the value of the company erodes even further. They must sell the firm for as much cash as possible and then seek out new opportunities. This situation can result from failing to develop new management talent or under-investing in the business. The result is that the business strengths needed are simply not present. Selling a family business without good market opportunities and the strength to capitalize on new ventures protects what remains of the family's investment. Continuing can only erode the family's and the company's capital further. The most logical strategy might be to invest that capital in financial assets, such as equities, bonds, or real estate.

Partnership for strategic business leadership

Beyond the tangible roadmap for the business there is another important outcome from this strategic planning process: shared understanding among the key actors in this important activity. The CEO and the management team, in collaboration with the chair and the board, form an important partnership. Their interaction represents shared ownership of the plan that leads to increased commitment. This commitment, especially on the part of the board, can take the form of support and encouragement for the management during the implementation process. The board's belief in the plan and willingness to endorse it in front of the family and other stakeholders is invaluable.

The relationship between the board, owners, and other stakeholders is also important, as the board represents their interests as well as those of the business itself. The board's engagement in the process of developing a strategy means that the owners and other stakeholders are actively represented in planning and decision making. They thus have a genuine input rather than being an afterthought or providing a rubber stamp. The owners can also see the board as championing the family's interest, as well as being a counterbalance to management control over the planning process.

The benefits of strategic business planning to key stakeholders far outweigh the extra time and investment it requires. Strategic business planning:

■   encourages management to act professionally and with responsibility

- stimulates a shared perspective of the business' possible future
- applies a systematic approach to analyzing the company as a whole
- facilitates the setting of objectives
- reveals future opportunities and threats
- provides a framework for decision making throughout the company
- analyzes and challenges the company's current position and plans
- clarifies the company's market position and competitive environment
- helps focus the efforts and energies of the entire organization.

The family's financial investment decision

An important step of the family business planning process, after determining the Strategic Direction, and the implementation tactics and actions, is to determine the level of investment required. At this stage, the strategic priorities and scenarios are discussed because investment levels are driven by the firm's Strategic Potential and business strategy. A firm with strong potential for value creation offers a high probability of an above-average return on investment. The firm's strategy also dictates or influences the level of investment required. A firm with an industry consolidation or high-growth strategy requires more financial investment than a firm that is in a steady market and milking the business for profits. In general, high-potential businesses simply need more capital. As noted, it is management that initially drives the planning process, while the board of directors oversees the process and its outcome. However the board, together with the owners, serves the vital function of deciding the firm's financial structure and its debt, dividend rate, and capital expenditures.

The question of investment brings us back to Sally. What should she do about her dilemma? There is no single answer or magic wand, but the insights from this chapter should help Sally to make her own judgment. By fitting her own family business into each of the models described above, she will gain a better understanding of the management's proposals to reduce the dividend. And if – after all that – she has not made up her mind how to proceed, the final step of the planning process is covered in Chapter 7, "Investing for family business success."

WHEN FAMILY BUSINESSES ARE BEST

- Developing a strategic plan is a process not an event. It helps the key stakeholders work together to develop a shared understanding of their situation and options.
- A well-crafted business plan provides a framework for decision making that is based on the family's vision and values.
- The business strategic plan cannot cover every future contingency or event that the family business will face, but rather guides the company's actions to planned events-and reactions to unforeseen circumstances.
- Family owners are a competitive advantage if they understand and support the business strategy.

7 Investing for Family Business Success

Family Actions

Business Actions

We have all heard the old maxim about how the first generation makes it, the second generation protects it, and the third generation spends it. Around the world there are similar expressions to communicate this three-generation pattern of business growth, investment maturity, and harvest: shirt sleeves to shirt sleeves, camel to camel, stable to stable, clogs to clogs, rice paddy to rice paddy. In other words, members of the third generation end up where their grandparents started, unless they do something special – like invest. The fact is that very few firms, whether family controlled or widely traded, survive for more than 50 years or three generations.

Investment decisions dictate the financial resources available to support the strategy, which is a critical factor in strengthening the business as it moves through the three-cycle pattern described above. The financial capital available, whether in the form of reinvested profits, debt, or new equity, determines the type and scope of business strategy the firm can pursue. Entrepreneurs and owner-managers are also psychologically "invested" in their business because it represents their career, wealth, and passion. The founder and even his or her children seldom struggle over the balance between reinvestment and dividends because it is assumed that earnings and cash flow support growth or acquisitions.

The power of the founder's global commitment to the business is validated by some recent research conducted by Professors Villalonga and Amit,[1] which shows that the firm's financial performance declines when the founder no longer serves as CEO or chairperson. This typically occurs at the time when the family shareholder group expands and the management and ownership roles are separated. At this point the unity of purpose about strategy and investment is complicated by competing demands for dividends, bonuses, family payouts, or increased liquidity. Planning and deciding together on the firm's financial structure is one method of helping business families focus a diverse ownership group on decisions about investment.

Throughout this book two forms of family investment are empha- sized: financial and human capital. Individuals' roles as executives, directors, active owners, members of the family council, or trustees of the family foundation represent the investment of human capital. When qualified family members serve in ownership or leadership roles they strengthen the business' ability to act and mobilize its stake- holders around critical decisions and actions including investment. Ugo Gussalli Beretta of the famous Italian firearms company summed up the issue of family investment when he said: "The temptation to make too much money out of the business was the greatest danger. We not only had our money, but also our hearts in the business."[2]

This chapter focuses on the financial investment of profits or other financial capital for the continued growth of the business (the devel- opment of human capital was covered in Chapter 5). How to manage the investment, distribution, or harvesting of financial capital is a dilemma faced by most family ownership groups as they consider the economics of their family businesses objectively. Families are orga- nizations, and as they grow in size and complexity, their need for a planning process to coordinate investment and ownership thinking becomes critical. The family business, after the first generation of the owner-entrepreneur, is driven by the demands of the family around their decisions about four generic ownership strategies: invest, hold, harvest, or sell (see Figure 7.1). Each of these strategies reflects the owners' investment commitment based on the business' potential for value creation and the family's commitment to the business.

Figure 7.1 *Aligning the family expectations and business demands to create business and investment strategies*

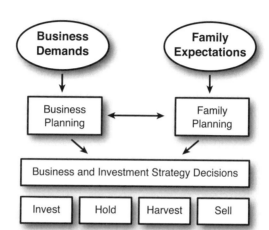

HOW DOW JONES WAS STARVED OF INVESTMENT

Often financial discussions do not lead to any real decision, and the business continues without an improved strategy or new investment plans. This is partially what happened to the Bancroft family introduced in Chapter 1. The story of Dow Jones could have been very different if the Bancrofts had been able to communicate a shared vision to the management and board about their expectations for their company (beyond quality journalism). This is also where the investment of human and financial capital could have played a major role. If the Bancroft family had been more active as directors and governing owners, they could have contributed to the development of the business strategy based on exploiting new opportunities and financial investment scenarios.

The Bancroft family's voting control gave them the ultimate accountability for ensuring that the management's strategy and implementation were creating value. But instead of becoming a competitive advantage, the family seems to have abdicated responsibility. The consequence was family stalemate and destruction of the Bancrofts' economic capital. In the end the family sold out to Rupert Murdoch despite their distaste for his journalism and commercial practices.

The case of the Bancrofts clearly demonstrates the need for a more rigorous approach to decision making for family investment. For 20-plus years the Bancrofts had debated the future, as the Dow Jones Company missed out on new opportunities and the family members' growing need for liquidity went unmet. While one of the issues blocking the Bancroft family was the senior generation's belief in their family's journalistic legacy, it is clear that they probably also lacked the tools to have an informed discussion about the strategic and investment issues facing their family business.

The logical outcome of discussing business strategy, new opportunities, and family investment is that the key actors – that is, the family owners, management team, and board of directors – think about long-term value creation. The owners are affected by the management's strategic plans and the management is affected by the family's investment decision. The board should play a central role in reviewing the strategy and confirming the dividend levels and the reinvestment rate. Some owners allow the board full authority, others advise the board and management of their wishes, and in some cases the family leaders make the decisions themselves. In practical terms the decisions must involve all three groups to ensure that the business and family are working toward the same goals and vision. If the managers choose an aggressive growth plan based on large capital expenditure but the owners seek liquidity and low risk, conflict is inevitable.

This rest of this chapter explores the challenges family business face about the family's investment of financial capital – and the resulting impact on the business' strategy and future ownership. The investment of human capital is implicit, even if it is not discussed. The two types of investment are closely related because, if the family are not able or willing to contribute leadership through active participation as owners, directors, or executives, then there is limited opportunity for them to be a positive force in contributing to the business' progress. A family that approve management and board actions after the fact, without taking an active role in investment and strategy decisions, do not add value to the planning process for the business – or for the family.

Many families practice a passive form of investment decision making because it is difficult to address the issues of maintaining control, generating investment capital, and providing returns or liquidity to the shareholders. Automatically reinvesting in a "legacy business" that your family founded and owns often appears to be a responsible and prudent decision. Legacy businesses have an established track record and the owners know what to expect. The family also feels a strong emotional tie to the business through their ancestors and sense of responsibility for the business' continued success. Unfortunately, this is not always a formula for sustaining wealth or family harmony, especially in a growing family and turbulent global marketplace.

THE INVESTMENT DILEMMA

Financial investment is a challenge for even the most capable and active business family because it involves making difficult decisions about competing demands that dramatically shape the future of the family's wealth, ownership, and relationships. Consider the Cargill family story from earlier in the book. When a group of Cargill family shareholders requested increased dividends, 125 years of ownership by the Cargill and MacMillan families had to be totally rethought. If the owners had decided to increase the dividend the company would have had less capital to invest and would be smaller and less profitable today. The option of selling Cargill stock to create liquidity for the family shareholders also had a downside: family control would have been eroded and the owners would have been forced to deal with outside investors and the stock market, probably with different goals and time frames. The last alternative was to do nothing – in which case the family shareholders would be locked together with golden handcuffs. The minority interested in a larger payout would have expressed their frustrations by criticizing the management, the board, or their relations, leading to conflict and a lack of focus on protecting the business' future.

Balancing these three variables of control, family liquidity, and business capital investment is what Francois de Visscher, a family business advisor and board member, calls the "family business investment dilemma," shown in Figure 7.2.[3] This diagram clearly demonstrates the conflict between managing the family's expectations and meeting the business' demands, which the Cargill-MacMillan family experienced in real life. It is also important to remember that the competing demands of liquidity, growth, and control all represent valid business goals. Owners expect dividends from their investment, management teams require capital to execute their strategies, and business families prefer to maintain private control of their firms.

A business family must, however, recognize that making a generational transfer of ownership and sustaining a growing business require

Figure 7.2 *Balancing control, liquidity, and capital needs*

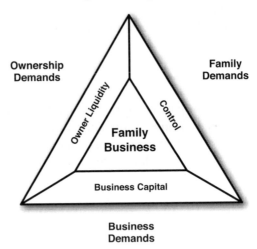

Suggested by F. M. de Visscher, C. E. Aronoff and J. L. Ward, *Financing Transitions: Managing Capital and Liquidity in the Family Business* (Atlanta: Business Owners Resources, 1995). Reprinted by permission.

new assumptions about debt, control, dividends, and compensation. In the early years, entrepreneurs and owner-managers typically reinvest all of the funds generated by the business in anticipation of future returns. As a result, the business consumes all or most of the available capital. As the family group grows, however, there are increasing demands on the business' financial assets. Eventually, the highest priority for a business family becomes its own financial security and liquidity needs. Unfortunately, without careful planning, that need for liquidity may result in insufficient capital for business growth.

Another issue that complicates the strategy and investment planning is that the senior generation often seek to retain control of the decisions, even when they are no longer running the business. Serious conflict can result when the next generation or non-family executives develop strategic plans that the senior generation will not support. In some families, succession and strategic planning are both blocked by the senior generation as they focus almost exclusively on retaining control. Unfortunately, however, that choice deprives the business of the resources it needs, and next-generation members of the opportunity to develop their careers and become effective business leaders.

BUSINESS CAPITAL NEEDS

There is no doubt that satisfying the financial demands of the business is a significant challenge to family business growth and even survival. Luc Darbonne, president of Groupe Darégal, a French global leader in frozen herbs, sums up his own situation:

> The main problem is that the business is limited by the capital. I'm in a niche market, but I'm a world leader. In order to grow, I need to invest everywhere on the globe and I can't do that without making a huge profit – which is hard in France. That's my main challenge.

Creating a business that is strong enough to compete successfully and support the needs of the family is the ultimate goal. But most families will have to make certain choices in an effort to minimize the constraints that stem from the competing capital demands. In order to complete the transfer of control and also to realize the Strategic Potential of the business, the owners will probably choose one or a combination of tactics (see Figure 6.3).

The Cargill and Wates families (introduced in Chapters 2 and 5 respectively) both developed strategies to address the investment dilemmas discussed here – and remained the controlling shareholders of successful businesses. Cargill created an employee ownership trust to buy out family shareholders, and the Wates used a leveraged buyout to buy back the stock of two family branches. Some other approaches to consider include:

- *Restructuring the family assets.* Separating ownership of the business from ownership of its real estate or other tangible assets can support different family expectations. This approach allows the operating business and its resulting profit stream to be sold or given to actively involved family members, while other assets and their associated cash flows offer a passive income for other family members.
- *Taking on more debt to provide capital.* Increasing the amount of debt can serve one of two purposes. The business can go into debt in order to finance new strategic developments. Or the borrowed funds may be used to buy out shareholders and help them finance

their estate plans and personal needs. In the latter case, debt is effectively used to retire or redeem ownership and to pass control to successors within the family through a leveraged family buyout.

■ *Joint ventures.* Partnering with other businesses to leverage resources and capabilities to exploit new opportunities without assuming all of the risk or investment.

■ *Divesting selectively.* The business may divest itself of one part of the company or of under-utilized assets. In effect, the choice is made to shrink the business in order to fund the buyout of certain family members and thereby maintain the rest of the family's ownership.

Discussing the family's needs for liquidity and control demonstrates the inevitable interdependence between the family's ownership and strategic business planning. The issue of ownership is never a certainty – especially if the senior generation are reluctant to cede control. And this, along with other uncertainties, can delay strategic planning. While the *Parallel Planning Process* cannot resolve all of the emotional issues, including that of control, it does help to put them into focus and provide the tools to drive an investment decision. Some of these tools, discussed below, can work even under difficult family conditions.

FAMILY BUSINESS COMMITMENT AND OWNERSHIP

Family commitment has two dimensions: first, *intentions* (the family's espoused values and vision) and second, *behavior* (the family's actions with respect to its investment of human and financial capital). Most business families describe themselves as "committed" to owning their family business but are challenged by conflicting demands to align their intentions and behavior. Consider, for example, a family business experiencing open conflict among the next generation or resistance from the senior generation to planning for ownership and leadership transitions. In such – all too common – cases the family usually espouses the continuity of family ownership but does not support it with its behavior.[4]

There are in fact four possible ownership strategies for business families, reflecting different levels of commitment (see Figure 7.3). As described in previous chapters, the family's ownership commitment is driven by the family's values and vision and also reflects the business' Strategic Potential. Family owners can Invest, Hold, Harvest, or Sell their holdings based on family needs and expectations.

The family's ownership strategy is influenced by the business' future prospects as expressed by its Strategic Potential. High-potential businesses will encourage investment and low-potential businesses will favor disinvestment. The Invest and Hold strategies represent an investment commitment at a high to medium level, whereas a Harvest decision would represent a medium investment level with the intention of creating long-term liquidity for the family. The Harvest strategy reflects the belief of some business families that they should diversify their wealth or reduce their business ownership because of changing family demands.

Sometimes market conditions may dictate the sale of a family business. Philip Blackwell, principal of Blackwell Ventures, describes how his family publishing business was eventually sold:

> Strategically the future for the publishing business was either "eat lunch" or "be lunch." But every potential large acquisition sold for 30 to 40 percent more than we thought it was worth. Eventually the penny dropped that we were probably worth more than we thought too. Other factors combined in a perfect storm too. There were external threats to the academic publishing

Figure 7.3 *Family business ownership strategies in relationship to strategic potential*

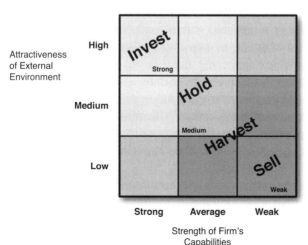

business model, the significant shareholders were all of a certain age and the excellent management team had reached the end of a business plan cycle. Then we found a buyer which was a natural fit – family controlled and with similar values.

The only pure disinvestment strategy is to sell the family holdings, and this typically occurs when the family or market conditions create an opportunity to sell profitably or the business faces threats from strong competitors, a mature industry, or management succession. These threatened businesses can also offer great returns, but require significant human and financial investment, as well as running a high risk of failure. Some families may choose to continue to support weak businesses for emotional or legacy reasons, but again this decision should be discussed openly so that everyone understands the motivations for continuing the family's investment.

Balancing conflicting demands

The decision about the family's rate of investment or disinvestment involves many subsidiary decisions, including how to use earnings and cash flow, whether to add new capital, and how to deploy debt. But in general terms, the old expression "money talks" is a good test of commitment. Simple logic suggests that a committed family will support the firm by reinvesting and forgoing current financial rewards for the long-term success of the business. Conversely, an uncommitted family or a business with a weak Strategic Potential will result in reduced investment, or possibly the sale of the business.

Three variables shape the family's investment: the management's business strategy, the business' Strategic Potential, and the family's commitment. The area of overlap among these variables will determine the family's investment decision. A firm with a large overlap has more strategic options. A firm with a small overlap or none at all may have no viable options other than reducing investment or selling the business.

Consider the case of a new venture founded by an entrepreneur. The entrepreneur has identified the opportunity and believes in its Strategic Potential; he or she has crafted the business strategy and is personally committed to implementing it. It is only logical that business founders decide to commit all of their talent and resources into their start-ups. In other words, the investment decision is fully supported by strategic potential, personal commitment, and the implementing the strategy.

Now consider the investment decision of a successful three-generation business family. The business is 43 years old and profitable, but is in a mature market with several major competitors, which have begun outsourcing their manufacturing to Asia. As a result, profit margins on domestically produced products are shrinking. The family has 26 members, aged from 2 to 81. Three of them work in the business as executives and one serves as chair of the board. There are 22 family shareholders, with no single person holding more than 6 percent of the voting shares.

Comparing the sole entrepreneur's and the large family's investment decisions, it is clear that they are very different. The entrepreneur's decision is made automatically: "This is my business!" The family's investment decision requires communication and planning to balance conflicting expectations and needs. Some members will expect an increase in their dividend, while others may think that they should perhaps sell their holdings because they have no career connections to the business. Another group may support the management's plan to sell off assets and redeploy capital in new markets. The investment decision that meets these competing demands is in a smaller range of possibilities than that of the sole entrepreneur (see Figure 7.4).

The family's investment decision determines how to fund the management's strategic plan while also providing payouts to the owners. As discussed in Chapter 6, the management begins its strategic thinking by reviewing the firm's competitive situation, identifying opportunities and then developing a strategic approach for aligning the business and new opportunities. For example, as already discussed, a firm with a strong Strategic Potential could consider a Market Leadership approach and develop a strategy of acquisition or joint ventures in new markets. If the owners believe in the potential of an acquisition or a new market to create economic value, they will work with the board to approve the plan and determine the level of financial investment required. They will also invest time and energy to learn more about the new opportunity and to show their support to management.

Figure 7.4 *Family investment: maximizing the overlap for three key variables*

Family business investment decisions

In reality, all businesses need to make investment decisions. It is unusual to find an operating business that does not need to invest some resources in updating technology, training employees, developing new products or markets, or improving facilities. Family investment is particularly important because it represents a shared vision of the future. A high-potential business owned by a committed family will invest the financial resources and leadership to fully exploit its potential. At the other extreme, a challenged business with uncommitted family owners can sell the business and use the family's assets for other purposes. The tough decisions involve all the family businesses in between these two extremes that need to carefully consider investment versus dividend or pay out decisions.

The *Family Business Investment Matrix* (see Table 7.1) is a simple tool for strategy and investment decisions that creates a framework for developing a dialog among the management, the board and the shareholders. It is never easy for families to discuss money because of the many socially constructed meanings that money has for families. Different family members may see money as power, control, rewards,

Table 7.1 *Family Business Investment Matrix*

A Business strategic potential	B Family commitment	C % of funds reinvested	D % dividend rate
Strong	Invest	60–100%	0–40%
Medium	Hold	40–60%	40–60%
Medium	Harvest	10–40%	60–90%
Weak	Sell	0	100%

recognition, security, philanthropy, love, care, or simply a tool for building a business.

The *Investment Matrix* is a decision-making template designed to take "some" of the emotion out of the investment decision and instead to turn it into a more objective exploration of the relationship between the business' Strategic Potential and the family's commitment. Instead of an unstructured discussion of personal views and feelings about investment, the family can use the management's assessment of the firm's Strategic Potential and their recommended strategies as input for the matrix. If there is agreement on the business' potential and the level of investment required for the management's plan, then clarifying family commitment becomes the critical issue in determining the level and source of capital for investment. The *Family Business Investment Matrix* does not recommend a specific investment or dividend rate but rather offers a range as a tool to help families engage in a meaningful discussion – following on from previous discussions about vision and commitment.

The *Family Business Reinvestment Matrix* offers four investment scenarios based on different combinations of Strategic Potential and Family Commitment. Column A in Table 7.1 represents the Strategic Potential of strong, medium, and weak businesses, in terms of their ability to create value for their owners. Column B represents the Family Commitment in terms of the stated intentions for continued family ownership. The family can Invest, Hold, Harvest, or Sell – representing a high to low commitment respectively. These two columns interact to influence the family's final decisions about investment and dividends.

Columns C and D represent the reinvestment and dividend decision, and are reciprocal unless there is outside funding such as debt or selling of new stock. The business' operating income funds the owners' dividends and the business' retained earnings.

Consider a business with a medium Strategic Potential and an owning family that has decided to Harvest some of its investment in the family business. This family would decide on a dividend of 60 to 90 percent and a reinvestment of 10 to 40 percent of funds. The Harvest scenario requires most of the firm's available operating cash flow, allowing more than half to be paid out to the family owners. Needless to say, the percentages are merely illustrative propositions. The guidelines in this table are also greatly affected by the requirements of the business and the industry for fixed and working capital, and by whether the business is increasing or decreasing its use of debt.

Overall, the idea of the matrix is to demonstrate the different reinvestment scenarios that result from the interaction of Strategic Potential and Family Commitment. Family shareholders need to consider these factors and understand the following implications for family business planning:

- Family businesses that require high levels of reinvestment need a high level of Family Commitment.
- Family members who express uncertainty or low commitment to the business should be offered a chance to sell their shares.
- If the family does not have a strong commitment to the business, a strategy should be developed to sell or harvest.
- There is an inherent conflict between low-commitment owners and a capable management team in a high-potential business. Low-commitment owners are not interested in high levels of reinvestment and, consequently, their actions limit the business' potential. Family or non-family managers who are not allowed to pursue business opportunities that support their career goals become frustrated. This frustration results in business disputes, family conflicts and eventually the loss of management talent. The loss of talented management reduces the firm's capabilities and affects its competitive position and financial performance.

- Business families can become dependent on payouts from the business (such as bonuses and dividends) and resist reinvesting for the business' future. This can result in failing to reinvest adequately, which means that the future generations will inherit a business poised to fail.

Most business families could benefit from a more rigorous approach to making decisions about family investment of their human and financial resources. This was a challenge for the Bancrofts. Even their own *Wall Street Journal* reported on the family's lack of ownership direction and internal conflicts: "The dissension was quashed 20 years ago and again 10 years ago, but this time it could not be ignored, as even older members of the family had developed doubts about the company's performance."[5]

The younger Bancroft family members realized the need either to sell the business or to support and fund a reformulation of the strategy into new markets like financial information. But the lack of consensus on investment and ownership resulted in the family business being sold for less than it had been worth ten years earlier – to a competitor whose values the family found distasteful.

Investment or disinvestment decisions are critical because they have an impact on so many family concerns: individual lifestyles, wealth creation, business competitiveness and strategy, family legacy, and psychological attachment. The owners' decision about how much of the firm's profits should be reinvested versus paid out to shareholders enables a business strategy to move from planning into implementation. The investment level and dividend policy is not a one-off discussion but rather an ongoing dialog among the owners, board, and management. Throughout that dialog, however, one fact of business life should always be remembered: it is prudent to keep a relatively low payout rate or to have some capital liquidity set aside so that cuts in investment are not required during tough economic times – and the business' value can be preserved.

WHEN FAMILY BUSINESSES ARE BEST

- Aligning the family business potential with financial and human capital creates an improved opportunity for value creation.

- If the family does not have a strong commitment to the business, a plan should be developed to sell or harvest the business.
- Misalignment between family commitment and business strategy can create conflict within the family or between the family and the management.
- Failing to reinvest adequately means that the future generations will inherit a weaker business.

Part IV

Family and Business Governance

8 Family Business Governance and the Role of the Board of Directors

Family Actions

Values >> Vision >> Strategy >> Investment >> Family meetings & agreements / Board of directors

Business Actions

Our management board has served us well. It was their support that helped us grow the company into one of the largest trading companies in the Gulf region. But the situation at our family business is changing and we need more expertise about management succession, ownership structures and global business strategies.

Waleed Al Said

Ten years ago when Waleed Al Said, aged 68, became CEO of the World Trading Company, he organized a management board that included: his older brother Hammad, 72, the former MD, as chairman; his younger brother Hussam, 64, a sales director for the last 20 years; Khaled, a cousin, 59, chief accountant in the firm; and two non-family employees, the commercial director, aged 58, and finance director, aged 66.

These characters are fictional, but the situation is typical of real life. Waleed's biggest concern is planning the next generation's leadership and ownership: there are six next-generation family members employed in the firm and eleven potential owners. He also wonders if the family's charitable work needs to become more professional. His daughter, aged 37, has been informally coordinating family charitable activities and last year distributed over $450,000 to 49 organizations and individuals. Another matter, which the current board seldom addresses, is the family's growing investments outside of the operating business that Waleed's cousin Khaled manages in addition to being the firm's accountant. The investments include real estate, private bank funds, financial instruments, and hedge funds.

"The next-generation executives employed by the firm are doing a great job but how do we decide on who should replace me as the next CEO?" Waleed asks. He would like to see his eldest son, aged 46, succeed him, but is also aware that his younger brother Hussam has aspirations to be the CEO – even though he has never demonstrated the required leadership performance.

Another potentially more difficult issue is the transfer of ownership to the next generation. Hammad believes that ownership should be based on Sharia law and that the entire next generation should inherit accordingly. Waleed believes ownership and employment must be tightly linked to protect the business, and strongly opposes ownership by all of the next generation, as only two of his children work for the firm. There are a total of 11 next-generation members, all of them married and many with children. The ownership decisions that the three brothers make will therefore have an impact on the long-term future of the entire family, not just on the business and its governance challenges.

The brothers have never directly discussed it, but all three are concerned about the potential for disputes among their children. They have seen too many families racked with conflicts that have destroyed family relationships and left a legacy of disharmony.

Waleed knows that developing an effective board is a starting point to improving his family's decision making and accountability for the business. He also knows that this will be a challenge, because both his brothers prefer the current family-dominated model of governance that has always worked so well for them. Waleed has several questions related to designing a board of directors for his family business and drafting family agreements. He also realizes that the family needs to start thinking longer term about how it plans and monitors its non-business investments and charitable activities.

THE CHALLENGES OF FAMILY
BUSINESS GOVERNANCE

Governance of a family-controlled business is fundamentally different from that of a widely traded firm because private ownership and family relationships can shield non-performing firms from public scrutiny and market pressures. Claude Janssen, honorary chair of INSEAD and chair of the International Council, emphasizes this point:

> Governance is critical for decision making in business families, especially if the family is the controlling shareholder. Building a board of family and independent directors, who are willing to put pressure on the family, is critical. The independent directors add a different perspective and counter the family's dominance to create more accountability.

Business families need parallel governance structures to support more effective decision making and strengthened accountability in their business management and family relationships. On the one hand, the board's role is to govern the business by supporting the creation of sound strategies, monitoring the firm's performance, and ensuring that it has capable leadership. On the other hand, family meetings and agreements encourage planning, support engagement, and ensure fairness in all kinds of family dealings. In addition, a trusted board often provides support for the family when it is facing important decisions on succession, investment, and other matters. Luc Darbonne, president of Groupe Darégal, a French global leader in frozen herbs, points out the added value to the CEO: "It can be lonely at the top of a company. You need a mirror to help you reflect, people who can give you a variety of answers. The more answers you have, the more solutions there are – and the better you sleep."

Family governance is a much more complex topic than business governance because – unlike company boards – there are no statutory or legal requirements. The family's involvement means that its governance structures and processes are shaped by its values, demographics and relationships. As the business family grows in size and complexity, its members need to strengthen their communication with planned family meetings or, in the case of larger groups, a family council. The family council is created when the family grows too large or geographically dispersed for all its members to meet together easily on a regular basis. Family council meetings serve as a "board" for the family and focus on effective family relationships by improving communications, providing a forum for planning and decision making, and creating more family accountability.

This chapter provides an overview of *business* governance in family firms. However, this cannot be separated from *family* governance, as we shall see. Governance is fundamental to the *Parallel Planning Process* because it helps families recognize the need for complementary governance structures, especially the board of directors and family council. Governance is also a tool for ensuring that the *Parallel Planning Process* results in continuous improvements for the family and business. This chapter specifically explores how the board of directors supports business and family planning and the family's investment decisions. Chapter 9 will further discuss *family* governance, including family meetings and agreements.

In the meantime, let's return to the Al Said family, which is facing critical decisions about issues that its current governance and ownership structures are not in a position to address. The family's board, dominated by family members and employees, has helped the brothers address business issues and decisions, but has not helped them deal with family concerns like Hussam's aspirations to be the next CEO.

The Al Said family is typical of successful family businesses struggling with important decisions and desperately trying to balance the needs of the senior and next generations. The three brothers have always worked as sibling partners, accepting each other's strengths and weaknesses, and avoiding tough decisions and issues. Their 11 children will not have the same natural connection, and this fact – combined with different educational backgrounds, personal aspirations, life experiences, and understanding of the family's values – creates the potential for conflict, misunderstanding, and disinterest. What the family needs to recognize is that their current decisions are secondary; first they need to agree on parallel governance processes that not only support the decisions they make now, but also create a foundation for family and business governance in future generations.

THE EVOLUTION OF FAMILY BUSINESS OWNERSHIP

A family business begins with at least one entrepreneur, who takes the owner-manager-director role (see Figure 8.1). Governance is not a

Figure 8.1 *The founder model of governance and management*

priority in the Owner-Manager stage, because founder-entrepreneurs are concerned with launching and building the business, and they do not see the need for involving others in their planning or decision-making activities. Their entrepreneurial style is based on a high need for control and low need for social support, so they prefer informal controls and maintaining a high level of personal involvement on all aspects of their venture.

As the founder's children (Sibling Partners) marry and start families and begin to take leadership roles in the business the need for more formalized governance activities becomes evident. It is during the Sibling Partnership stage that the nature of the ownership group can first change with the separation of ownership and management roles as some siblings becoming just owners. This evolution of ownership eventually develops into five possible different ownership roles each with different motivations and expectations of any governance structures that may exist (see Figure 8.2).

During the Sibling Partnership stage the separation of roles, the increasing complexity of the business, and the expanding family size means that informal work discussions and shared authority need to be replaced with governance structures like a board of directors, shareholder agreements, and family meetings. Also, as the business professionalizes, informal governance is no longer effective for planning and decision making, with highly trained executives and a board of directors that may include outsiders.

The Cousin Collaboration and Family Enterprise stages increase the need for more formalized governance, as a larger number of family members and in-laws often have reduced connections to the business and weaker family relationships. The reduction of the family's emotional connection – often labeled psychological ownership – occurs when a larger number of the family members did not grow up with the founder or close to the business. Some cousins will have parents who did not work in the business; other cousins will have non-business careers and may not be very business literate. In-laws may also become involved based on their business expertise or marriage. No matter how it happens, there are almost inevitably an expanded number of family members who will function as different types of owners. During the Cousin Collaboration stage there is also often a growing interest in non-business activities such as family investments and philanthropy. It is at this stage that the family's need for more governance becomes apparent. Family meetings, written family agreements and a family council are usually established – and possibly a family office or foundation board too. The family's interest in non-business activities represents a shift away from governing owner and active owner roles, as the family's priority becomes planning and decision-making for itself and other activities rather than the business (see Figure 8.3).

The Cousin Collaboration and Family Enterprise stages usually

Figure 8.2 *The phases of family ownership and governance activities*

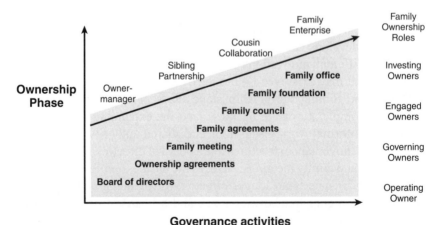

Figure 8.3 *Governing the family enterprise: moving beyond the operating business to multiple family activities*

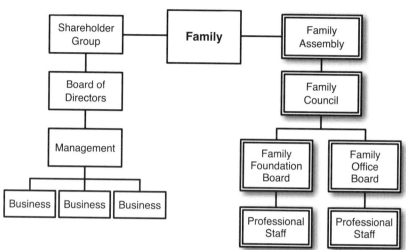

represents a definitive change in ownership type away from owner-manager or governing owner roles to active, investing, and passive owner roles. Often more family members are involved as board members of the family council, office, or foundation than as directors of the operating business. The business has grown and matured, and is led by professional family or non-family executives and board members. The increased number of family members from different branches and generations requires sophisticated family governance processes. The scale of the business and the size of the shareholder group make the situation similar to that of widely traded companies in many ways.

Consider the Wendel family with its 12 generations and over 1,000 shareholders. This 300-year-old French business family has more family shareholders than many public companies. Priscilla de Moustier, a family director who chairs their Comité Cohésion de Famille (Family Cohesion Committee), shares their story:

For 270 years the family was in the steel business in the Lorraine region of France. We survived the French revolution, the Franco-Prussian War, and World War One and Two only to see our company nationalized by the government in the 1970s. In one moment we lost our business and identity – and the strong sense of community that tied us to Lorraine.

Today, the family business has re-established and reinvented itself, but as Priscilla de Moustier puts it, "Our struggle is: how do we keep the family glue working with 1,000 family shareholders and growing larger?"

The Wendel family recognized that to sustain family commitment it needed to do more than issue reports on financial results and investment strategies. It therefore began a family awards program that demonstrates the family's values. Two financial awards recognize next-generation family members for entrepreneurial achievement and humanitarian projects. Knowing the importance of education and networking, the Wendels also developed a series of next-generation seminars on finance and family business ownership. They also established regular shareholder–board dinners with guest speakers for the senior generation. As Priscilla stresses, "maintaining strong family connections is the challenge."

At all ownership stages there is a possibility of finding passive owners who have limited interest in the business or its performance but remain owners for emotional or legacy reasons. Family owners can have an emotional connection simply because the business was once founded and led by their relatives. As the 82-year-old matriarch of Nash Engineering, a US-based family business that was owned by the same family for over 100 years old, commented, "I never thought of it as a special business, I thought of it as just family and that is what family does."[1]

PARALLEL FAMILY AND BUSINESS GOVERNANCE ACTIVITIES

Nowhere is the *Parallel Planning Process* more beneficial than in aligning family and business governance activities to make them mutually supportive. If a business family gets it right, governance will promote an ongoing dialogue between management and the family about family commitment and contribution on the one side and business strategy and performance on the other. An effective board, working with a capable management team and a well-functioning family, will focus its planning and actions on value creation and long-term ownership continuity. Family and business governance are clearly interrelated – the board monitors strategy and leadership planning, and thus supports the family's contributions of financial and human capital.

The board of directors – a legal requirement in most countries – is the primary governance structure for any family business. During the business' early stages the board is first, a legal entity for tax and other required statutory actions, and second, a sounding board for the owner-manager. It usually starts as an advisory board, comprised of trusted employees, professional advisors, such as the lawyer and accountant, or friends. This group meets informally with the owner-manager to discuss plans and decisions. As the business grows and ownership and management roles are separated, the board often becomes more formal and professional in its role: providing feedback, confirming the management's actions, considering succession, and assessing performance.

A board of directors is usually the first of the six generic structures that support family and business governance, as shown in Figure 8.4. They are displayed in a circular format because family and business governance activities do not follow a linear sequence. Some families may have a board of directors that unilaterally handles all governance activities, while others start with a board and then develop family agreements facilitated by the board. Ideally family and business governance should develop democratically so that a strong sense of family ownership based on participation is created.

- *Board of directors.* An effective board integrates and enhances the *Parallel Planning Process* in two fundamental ways. The board encourages planning and facilitates decisions that resolve critical business issues. In addition, strong outside directors bring a new level of accountability for actions taken by the business and family.
- *Shareholder agreements.* Ownership is relatively simple when the founder owns 100 percent of the stock in a partnership or corporation. It becomes more complicated when he or she considers options for passing ownership to his or her children, and decides to create legal structures to ensure continuity of family control, minimize taxes, or prevent family conflicts. Possible legal agreements include trusts, wills, foundations, voting agreements, and buy–sell contracts. Some families create legal entities such as holding companies, limited partnerships, trusts, or multiple classes of stock to structure ownership permanently.
- *Family meetings.* Family meetings are a part of everyday life in

Figure 8.4 *Family business governance activities*

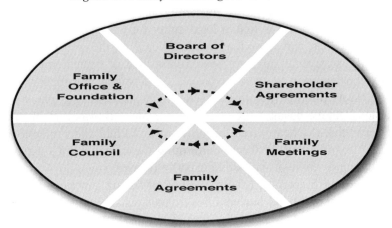

some family firms. In fact informal meetings can occur whenever family members are together for meals, holidays, or even religious events. As Vasiliki Anyfioti, an INSEAD MBA and next-generation family member, recalls, "I can't remember a meal or family gathering where business was not discussed." As the family grows, organizing regular family meetings with agendas becomes an important tool for maintaining communication and a sense of connection.

■ *Family agreements.* Also known as family "charters," "constitutions," or "protocols," these are ethical agreements among family members defining the rights, responsibilities, and relationships of family members with respect to each other and to the business. Such agreements typically set out values, a code of conduct, employment and compensation guidelines, procedures for handling conflicts, relationships with the board, family education, family council roles and responsibilities, philanthropy, and dividend and reinvestment policies.

■ *Family council.* The council formalizes family meetings, as the family group grows larger. The family council is a smaller representative group selected by the family to discuss issues and establish plans or policies for family actions. The family council works to build family unity and encourage the development of family talent and constructive participation.

■ *Family office and foundation.* These two structures help families
   manage assets and interests outside of the operating business.
   The primary role of the family office is to manage the family's
   financial assets and investments, and coordinate professional
   services such as financial planning, insurance, and legal or tax
   advice. Family offices also often support the work of the family
   council. Family foundations are created to plan and develop
   charitable initiatives.

A family business does not need to formalize all of the governance
structures described above. But most multi-generational firms of significant size need some such processes to fulfill the functions identified.
The combination of concentrated ownership, strong emotional connections, and an expanded set of activities demands that family-controlled
businesses have sound parallel governance structures that support the
alignment of often conflicting family and business goals.

Family business governance roles and responsibilities

The board of directors and family council – representing the shareholders
or business, and entire family, respectively – drive family business
governance. A family concerned about creating effective governance
structures needs to start by discussing the responsibilities and relationships of these two interrelated entities. This is a key advantage of the
Parallel Planning Process, which recognizes the need to coordinate the
relationship between business and family interests. Figure 8.5 shows
the family council and board as equal entities reporting to the family
assembly (annual family meeting) and shareholder group respectively.
These reporting relationships vary with different families, and this figure
is intended only to show that each business family needs to agree on the
relationship between the family council and board of directors – based
on family values and vision, and the type of owners. Some families
operate two parallel and equal entities, some will give the final say to
the family council, while others will defer to the business board.

No matter what the hierarchy or reporting relationship, the family
council and board of directors are often required to share information
or coordinate action because of the overlap in the family and business
systems. These groups may simply offer counsel to each other, or in

difficult situations, they may both be asked to participate in decision making. Sharing decisions and plans related to family agreements, ownership transfers, management succession, and business strategy ensure that the family and the business complement each other. The family council and board of directors are precisely the right parallel forums for that sharing planning while maintaining boundaries between family and business systems.

The role of the board of directors

The board is the foundation of any business governance because it has legally stipulated duties and responsibilities. The board represents the company's, employees', or owners' interests depending on the legal statutes of the country in which the business is registered. For example, in the United States the board traditionally represents the shareholders' interests; in the United Kingdom the business' interests; and in Germany the employees' interests. Globalization and improved thinking about governance has modified this pattern slightly. In most countries today, boards attempt to take a broad view of their responsibilities towards a range of stakeholders.

The corporation's board of directors is responsible for protecting the company's assets, ensuring that capable management is in place, and supporting strategies that create shareholder value. The board is elected or appointed by the shareholders, and legally directs – not manages – the corporation's actions. In a family firm, the board is typically comprised

Figure 8.5 *The fundamental family business governance entities*

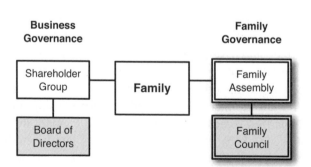

of family members and, in the best cases, experienced businesspeople from outside the company. Ideally the majority of directors, or at least three or four of them, will be independent and external. Luc Darbonne of Groupe Darégal believes in the importance of independence to the extent that he invites only outsiders to be directors: "My board is only outside people – mainly in their early sixties. People are very efficient in the early years of retirement! It's the board that makes all our main decisions."

The critical tasks of the board include:

■ monitoring the firm's performance and assessing the CEO
■ providing support and counsel to the senior management team
■ contributing to the strategic planning process
■ mentoring family employees on careers and development
■ linking family shareholders with the management team
■ representing the needs of non-family stakeholders.

In addition to its formal business roles, the board can also support the family's relationship with the business. As Redha A. Faraj, an independent family business board member from Bahrain, points out, "Independent directors are an important buffer to help focus family business discussions and decisions. The independent directors are there to help people see different sides of the issues." These independent directors provide a third perspective to counterbalance the views of the management and the family.

The independent board members can also play an invaluable role in planning and decisions about the businesses' future strategy. Faraj says:

> Often family owners are not technically trained in business so when they need advice their independent directors can contribute. Think about the life cycle of the business as an example. Family members see a successful business, so think, "Let's keep doing more of the same strategy." Independent directors need to remind them that some day the business will be mature and not be so profitable or competitive.

An effective board with independent members also demonstrates to the next generation that the family is committed to professionalism in ownership and management, as well as to new ideas.

The role of the family council

This is the family's "board of directors," representing the entire family and providing a governance mechanism for planning and mediating ownership, relationship, or career issues that arise from the overlap of business and family systems. The critical tasks of the family council include:

- reviewing and updating family agreements
- discussing and transmitting family values and a shared vision
- planning family activities for education, socializing, and relationships
- making family decisions and mediating conflicts
- working to professionalize the family's contribution to the business.

The family in large, multi-generational families often have limited family involvement in the business or interaction among family members. The family assembly (all "adult" family members and, in some families, in-laws) and shareholder group are not usually a functioning entities like a board or family council, but may meet annually to discuss and ratify the actions of the family council and board. The focus of the family assembly is on social and family actions and the focus of the shareholder group is on financial and business performance.

Board versus family council participation and responsibilities

The board's focus on business and management tasks – in contrast with the family council's focus on social, education, and relationship tasks – would logically indicate that the membership criteria are different. Figure 8.6 shows the differences and interrelationships between responsibilities and membership criteria of the family council, board of directors, and shareholder group. Business families face relationship issues, and the family council membership criteria requires representing the family; the board is about business performance, and its membership criterion is professional competence; ownership is about assets and value creation, and membership is based on owning stock.

Figure 8.6 *Family business governance responsibilities and membership criteria*

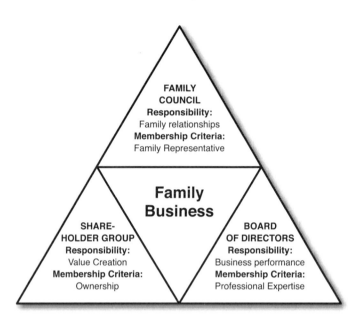

EFFECTIVE BOARDS OF DIRECTORS

The best family businesses have a strong team at the top, which includes a talented and motivated CEO, a respected and capable chair of the board, an experienced and involved board of directors, and committed owners. Effective governance is one of the family's most important tools for influencing the business, and can play an important role in several leadership scenarios. Governance can serve to support a strong family-led management team and ensure that the interests of all the family are well represented. If a non-family management team leads the business, the board can monitor performance to ensure that the family's interests and capital are protected. This section will explore the board's contribution to the overall success of the family and the business. However, the responsibility for selecting and empowering a capable and effective board of directors lies with the owners.

Family decisions on creating boards

Developing a functioning board, especially with outside directors, is often an outcome of the *Parallel Planning Process*. In working through earlier steps of the process, the family realizes that it needs improved discipline and accountability to support the family vision. It often becomes clear during family meetings that both the business and family owners would benefit from the creation of a board.[2] The discussion about creating a board should cover:

■ the board's role and decision-making authority
■ the composition of the board: management, family, and independent directors
■ the selection criteria, appointment process, and terms of office for board members
■ a method for evaluating the performance of the board and its individual members
■ the role of the chair of the board and its relationship to the role of CEO
■ compensation of board members.

A board, when well conceived and given clear authority and responsibility, is an invaluable tool. The opposite is also true. A board comprised of family members determined to counteract a strong CEO's authoritarian rule only creates another venue for conflict and negative feelings.

There may be some reluctance to authorize a board of directors with outside members or even younger members of the family. For this reason, some families choose to begin their governance activities with a board of advisors who provide a new level of objectivity, but without the formal or legal structure of a board of directors.

THE BOARD AND THE *PARALLEL PLANNING PROCESS*

The remainder of this chapter will briefly summarize how the board of directors contributes to the *Parallel Planning Process* developed throughout this book, and illustrate how an effective board can strengthen that process. The board helps the owning family and the management to affirm their commitment to business continuity. It also helps the family develop its thinking about participation and succession and investment. Finally, the board can bring great value to the management's development of a strategic plan for the business.

The board and family values

Many families draw on their boards as they develop and articulate their core values and family business philosophy. Asking only the family about its values often fails to identify the most distinctive beliefs and principles. Independent directors can see the family's history and behaviors through fresh and objective eyes. They can challenge the family to draft a values statement and a commitment statement that have greater richness and detail – and are both more compelling and more gratifying for the owners. This can make all the difference to the family's commitment to the business.

The board also can play a helpful role as the management explores its strategy. The board can challenge managers to be more focused in their view of the business, and to be more realistic and precise in their long-term goals. An important duty for any independent director is to ask challenging, thought-provoking questions of executives. When they do, good management teams appreciate the sharpening of their own thinking – and this supports strategy development within the *Parallel Planning Process*.

Finally, integrating the board into the early phases of the *Parallel Planning Process* can provide an excellent forum for representatives of both family ownership and management leadership to confirm a shared vision. If each party is supported in their exploration of the other's views there is more likely to be a full understanding and confident commitment on both sides.

The board and commitment of family ownership

As the family discusses its participation, the board can help in many very important ways – especially when the family firm is a private company. The directors can serve as a valuable sounding board for the family as it develops written agreements. Many families will write a draft agreement and ask the board for input on the business impact before finalizing their document. This helps ensure that the business perspective has been fully considered. Business families with independent directors who genuinely care about the family's growth and welfare are most fortunate. There is probably no resource that can objectively support a family's needs better than an effective board.[3]

The board also contributes indirectly to family governance and family planning by setting a professional standard in the business. Boards with independent directors provide a role model for others involved in planning and decision-making processes. Above all, boards help to ensure and enhance Fair Process, especially if they are invited to family meetings and become personally known to family members. Familiarity between the independent directors and the family owners can also be promoted by sharing agendas and minutes of meetings. Another simple technique is to schedule family and board meetings for the same day. The family or shareholders meet in the morning and have lunch with the board, which then holds its own meeting in the afternoon. The shared lunch creates an opportunity for interaction within the context of family and business governance activities.

As the family prepares the next generation for management and leadership, the board can help greatly. Directors can be mentors for members of the next generation as they progress in their careers. Directors can also provide networks of contacts for work and life experience beyond the family firm. Once the next generation is fully involved with the firm, the board can offer objective perspectives on policies and decisions about compensation. And, perhaps most valuable of all, the board can provide independent and respected feedback to family members on their job performance and personal development.

The board also has an important contribution to make to succession planning. One of the board's generic functions in any company is to work with the CEO to ensure that a qualified successor and senior team is developed. An independent board that is actively involved in the succession process can make decisions that are difficult or impossible for family members to make. Directors who are known and respected by the family make these decisions easier to accept, and can reduce unhealthy rivalry in the family.

Addressing the future ownership and estate plans of a family, as discussed in the next chapter, is often the most difficult of family situations. A trusted board serves as a catalyst and source of encouragement for the family to face these decisions. The board offers a powerful symbolic contribution; the mere existence of a board with independent directors demonstrates a commitment to professionalism. Independent directors also exemplify the family's commitment to practicing steward-ship. When a family goes to the effort to build an independent, outside board and voluntarily shares accountability with it, care for the interests of others and for the future of the business is reinforced for all to see.

The board and business strategy

Management teams in family businesses with strong boards have a special advantage. Kenneth Dayton, a family business executive and founder of the Target Stores in the United States, discussed in a 1984 *Harvard Business Review* article how good governance and good management are "two sides of the same coin." Never is this truer than when the board provides creativity and a fresh perspective for the formulation of strategy. In family-owned businesses such decisions must be made with long-term performance in mind.

As management does its SWOT analysis, as described in Chapter 6, a good board adds distinct value. Wise managers will share the prelimi-nary results of their internal capabilities assessment with the board. It is a well-accepted principle of strategic planning that management teams have a tremendous temptation to over-appreciate the company's strengths and under-appreciate its weaknesses, whether in their capa-bility analysis or their competitive analysis. Board members, however, can be objective.

The board also strengthens the management's efforts to scan the external environment as it works to determine the business' Strategic Potential. A diverse set of directors with a breadth of experiences bring new understanding of changes in the external environment. They may even have personal experience of the external trends and forces that are likely to influence the business.

In addition, the outside view of independent directors stretches managers' thinking on the definition of the industry and of the relevant competition. Globalization and forces such as new technology, changing social values, restructured economies, and the need for sustainable resources mean that businesses require new insights to support their planning. An experienced board can ask tough questions to challenge managers' assumptions and help them look at the business in new ways, so that they identify the right strategic options.

Last but not least, the board can be vital in helping the management to exploit the special competitive advantages that family ownership offers – and to avoid the common disadvantages.

The board and family investment decisions

Technically, in most jurisdictions, the board of directors sets the dividend (and corresponding reinvestment rate) based on their assessment of the business' capital structure and strategic needs. The *Parallel Planning Process* recognizes that reinvestment is the owning family's decision, but that they often rely on the board's advice and support. An independent board is the most logical group to assist in developing and monitoring the reinvestment analysis and decisions that are outlined in the Chapter 7. Directors can help the family to feel confident in its attitudes towards risk, confirming the management's assessment of the firm's Strategic Potential, and endorsing the family's final decision about reinvestment.

More specifically, the board is the most knowledgeable group available to explore the appropriate dividend–reinvestment ratio for a particular business and a particular family. In addition, the board has the best vantage point from which to advise on how the business' potential supports the family's long-term goals for value creation.

A final thought on the board and leadership and ownership succession

This book is about parallel planning for the family and business. We have deliberately not emphasized leadership and ownership succession, because our work with families suggests that it is more important to have good processes in place before addressing specific issues and challenges. However, we will close this chapter with a warning that the inability of the senior generation to "let go" can disrupt all the rational analyses generated by the *Parallel Planning Process*. Here again, an independent board can make a special contribution. Often the only people who can help the senior generation face the ambivalence and pain of succession are trusted board members.

As for Waleed Al Said, he is a fictional character based on several families, so we are free to give his story a happy ending. He took the essential, if initially troublesome, step of professionalizing his board and a few years later stepped down as CEO. Thanks to the board's insights, he and his family realized that Hussam (Waleed's younger brother) was not suited to the leadership role. Reluctantly, Waleed also came to recognize that his elder son was not up to the job. In fact, in an emotional showdown between father and son, mediated by one of the most trusted members of the new board, it transpired that the younger Al Said did not even want to be CEO. A non-family manager with excellent credentials was appointed to lead the business, and so far, they have all lived happily ever after. Waleed is now in the process of working with Hussam and his son to establish a family council.

This chapter has attempted to summarize the importance of good governance and to illustrate how an effective, independent board of directors can add special value to the *Parallel Planning Process*. The next chapter addresses the topic of family governance – the final step of the *Parallel Planning Process*. It is only with effective family governance that the business family can fully implement a planning process that addresses the needs of the family business system. Family governance lays the foundations for family harmony – financial, social, emotional, and spiritual. After all, there is more to life than business.

WHEN FAMILY BUSINESSES ARE BEST

- *Parallel Planning* for governance provides a comprehensive framework to align both management and owners in decision-making and ensuring accountability.
- An independent board is an invaluable tool to advise business families with their *Parallel Planning* activities including vision and investment.
- The board of directors, properly designed and led, supports management in the strategic planning processes.
- An effective board of directors is particularly helpful in times of transition.

9 Family Governance: Family Meetings and Agreements

Family Actions

Business Actions

The following newspaper report tells the story of a nightmare caused by weak family and business governance that allowed an ownership conflict to turn into a lawsuit that eventually led to a judge splitting the business' assets and ownership.

COURT ORDERS LIQUIDATION FOR CITY WAREHOUSE FIRM

A Ramsey County District Court judge ruled Thursday that Space Center Inc. should be placed in receivership and sold to resolve a long, bitter dispute among members of a family who control the St. Paul warehouse company.

Space Center was founded in 1916 as St. Paul Terminal Warehouse Co. by Harry McNeely Sr. (who died in 1968). The children are now fighting for control of the company. Donald G. McNeely, son of the company's founder, is chairman of Space Center, president of a holding company, and head of more than 40 subsidiaries. His brother, Harry McNeely Jr., is vice president of the holding company, and a director of Space Center. Together, they own a majority of the company's stock.

The two men are being sued by the minority shareholders, led by their own sisters. They argued in court that their brothers had frozen them out of the company's management and any significant share of the profits, and that the brothers were running the company for their own benefit. Specifically, the sisters claimed that the brothers had "avoided paying significant dividends, failed to disclose required information, and misused corporate assets for their own gain." None of the minority shareholders has served on the company's board.

The lawyer representing the McNeely brothers said, "If this decision of Judge Lynch is permitted to stand, it will be the demise of a company that provides jobs for 750 families. What we have here is minority shareholders who have lived most of their lives in Europe and just want to get money out of their holdings."

Source: Langberg, M. Court orders liquidation for city warehouse firm, *St. Paul Pioneer Press Dispatch*, November 1, 1985.

In 1916, Harry McNeely Sr. borrowed $5,000 – a great sum of money in that era – from his father-in-law to start a warehousing and transportation business in downtown St. Paul, the St. Paul Terminal Warehouse Co. Under the leadership of his two sons, Donald and Harry Jr., who joined in 1937 and 1949, the company grew over the succeeding decades by acquiring properties all across the United States – based on an opportunistic strategy that often combined the purchase of under-utilized real estate with the operation of a public warehouse or provision of third-party logistics services. By the time of Harry Sr.'s death in the late 1970s, the company, now called Space Center, was a large real estate group managing warehousing for some of the largest US companies.[1]

After the brothers had successfully managed the business for many years, the existence of Space Center was however threatened, not by any economic or competitive forces, but by a family discord that pitted the two brothers against their two sisters, who were minority owners. The two McNeely daughters, who did not work in the business, hired a law firm to contest their father's will, in which – unlike their brothers – they had received a cash settlement rather than shares in the business. Although they settled before going to court, with the daughters receiving a "gift" of shares in the business from their mother, there was trouble again some 15 years later. The sisters, as minority shareholders, once again took their brothers to court, arguing that they had been frozen out of the company's board and any significant share of the profits, and that the brothers were running the company for their own benefit. The result was the largest court-ordered, minority-shareholder business liquidation in Minnesota's history.

The consequences to the family and business were disastrous. After losing a bitter court battle, the brothers were forced to split off some of the company's holdings to pay the court judgment in favor of their sisters. The courtroom drama convinced Donald, the oldest brother, that he never wanted the family involved in his business interests again, whereas Harry Jr. still believed in the advantages of family ownership. These differences over the future vision resulted in the remaining family firm being again restructured into two separate holding companies, each led and owned by one of the brothers.

Not many family businesses survive this kind of tragedy. Yet somehow this experience galvanized Harry McNeely Jr. to rebuild his part of the business and renew the family's values and spirit. Harry Jr. determined that the second split was his opportunity to recreate a long-lasting family business. He continued the same business strategy, but with a new focus on the family values of fairness, participation, professional governance, social responsibility, and family commitment. His first step was to recruit a group of experienced outside executives to sit on a new board of directors – and support his goal of rebuilding the family business.

The new board of Meritex, formerly Space Center, included a majority of independent directors (a rarity at a time when family business boards were usually composed of family executives), the family accountant, and a lawyer and a good friend. Harry Jr. also asked each of his next-generation family members to serve a one-year term on the board to learn about governance firsthand.

From then on, whereas previous communication among relatives had been poor and partisan, good family communication became a priority. Family meetings were organized regularly. A family council was created, and still meets quarterly, to discuss the business with complete transparency. As Harry Jr. says, "Everyone knows everything and everyone contributes." He encouraged the development of family talent, with a particular focus on generational renewal, and educated his children to be effective owners and potential directors by sending them to leadership programs at well-respected business schools.

The family foundation was at the heart of this renewal for the extended McNeely family. Harry McNeely Jr. reached out to ensure that all his brothers' and sisters' children were included in the foundation, working together as his sibling generation was never able to do. Today, in addition to the foundation's work in education, the environment, the arts, and community betterment, it has also sponsored the development of a family business center at the University of St. Thomas in St. Paul to make education and advice available to others. In 2008 *Minnesota Business Magazine* named Harry Jr.'s company "Family Business of the Year." From the ashes of a court order requiring business liquidation, the McNeelys have rebuilt a successful business whose needs and aspirations are balanced with those of the family.

Harry Jr.'s experience with his brother and sisters helped him realize the importance of communication and of using family and business governance as tools for making decisions that support both business performance and family unity. When his oldest son, Paddy, returned to Meritex, ready to take on top-level operational responsibilities after working outside the company for ten years, it was the board of directors – supported by family meetings – that crafted a succession plan, which eventually led to his becoming CEO. As the issue of ownership transition to the next generation unfolded, Harry again relied on his board and family meetings to make plans and decisions that satisfied the needs of the family, business, and other stakeholders.

This case shows how the lack of effective family governance can have devastating effects on a family and business, and how – when it is properly applied – governance can support exceptional results. The McNeely family will always share the heartbreak of an unresolved family split (Donald never again spoke to his sisters) and a prolonged legal dispute. However, the positive outcome of the story is the resulting deep appreciation of governance activities in helping a family work together. Beyond rebuilding the business, Harry has also united the cousins from all of the family branches, including those that had sued, to serve on the board of the family foundation. Parallel planning to create sound family and business governance, based on core family values about working together, has enabled the third generation to continue their grandparents' legacy of service to others through philanthropy – and begin the process of transferring this legacy to the fourth generation.

At a recent international conference on family business, three generations of the McNeely family recounted their story. Perhaps the most touching moment was when Harry, now in his eighties, sat before an audience of family business members from around the world, listening proudly as his grandson shared their dreams and hopes for the McNeelys' future.

THE VALUE OF FAMILY GOVERNANCE

Most business families do not appreciate the positive contributions of effective family governance processes – developed in parallel with those of the business. Good family governance can improve communication, encourage fairness, and sustain commitment, all of which can only have a positive impact on the family firm.

Formal family governance also supports generational transitions by helping the generations engage with each other constructively in planning and decision making about the business' future. As the generations multiply and more people gain a stake in the business, conflict becomes more likely. Here again, family governance comes into its own as an important tool for reducing the consequences of interpersonal and family disagreement by creating agreed structures for planning and making decisions about critical issues. No matter how well a business family works together, eventually it will face tough decisions over personal relationships, business actions, emotional hurt, òr future plans – resulting in conflicts that cannot be resolved informally. Emotions will run high and differences will seem irreconcilable. At such points, structures such as family councils supported by clear written agreements are absolutely necessary.

A family that does not address conflict encourages a dynamic that is not open and honest. When family members feel that their disagreements over decisions, expectations, or relationships are not being addressed, tension builds up until the emotional pressure becomes too much, and it explodes in a destructive manner. Addressing conflicts in the family or business is always a difficult task, because no one enjoys confronting their loved ones over highly emotional issues. The next section offers suggestions on how to explore conflict and turn it around to become a tool for strengthening performance and relationships.

UNDERSTANDING FAMILY CONFLICT

Conflict is a natural part of human relationships, whether in a family or business setting. Conflict is neither positive nor negative; if handled correctly it leads to new thinking, better planning and decisions – and a stronger sense of trust and commitment. When two brothers disagree about an issue but agree to work together to discuss it and come to a mutually acceptable decision, they are building trust and strengthening their relationship. The same applies to other family groups which learn that difficult discussions can offer an opportunity to explore new perspectives and identify better possible solutions than if one person works alone.

Business families experience three main forms of conflict:

- *Issue conflict* is a part of almost every human interaction. When more than one person shares an idea, offers a plan, or makes a decision, there is potential for conflict because of different values, goals, and motivations. Issue conflict is a part of our daily lives, and we all have routines and heuristics to make its resolution part of our interpersonal relationships. These informal tools for conflict resolution work fine because the stakes are small and most people do not want a discussion about every issue they face. The problems occur when the stakes are large or the issue involves an emotional connection.
- *Process conflict* occurs when we lack the tools or structures to address an issue. If two cousins do not communicate and there are no family structures to help them resolve their differences, they will have an ongoing conflict. Process conflict occurs when a family has not developed effective interpersonal skills or governance structures to address the routine issues that confront them.
- *Relationship-based conflict* can occur in two forms, both equally damaging. The first form can result when a lack of effective processes allows a series of unresolved business issues between individuals or groups to destroy their trust in each other. This failure results in a pattern of unsuccessful interactions that block future attempts at working together. The second form of relationship conflict comes from an unresolved emotional injury that manifests itself as destructive behavior in personal interactions. In both these cases the individuals or groups involved disagree no matter what the issue, because they lack the trust or emotional insights to work with each other.

Conflict is an ongoing issue for business families because of the overlap of family and business systems – and the fact that they share lifetime relationships. This proximity often means that family disputes overshadow work and love, as the example of the McNeelys demonstrates. However, it is worth considering how good governance can help to reconcile business and family issues – supporting improved productivity for the business and stronger relationships for the family. Paddy McNeely, the current chairman and CEO of Meritex, describes governance as a life saver. "It provides clear separation between the owners and the business – as well as holding us together," he says.

Many families are afraid to address problems because they fear that simmering conflicts may explode. Manfred Kets de Vries, Chaired Clinical Professor of Leadership at INSEAD, warns that families often avoid honest and sometimes painful communication about the reality of their situation in the interests of maintaining the "myth" of familial harmony.[2] There is no question that maintaining harmony is important, but addressing conflict is crucial to the growth of individuals, family relationships, and the company.

Family values and traditional cultures are often a roadblock for more open and honest communication. Fred Tsao, sole owner of ICM, a Singapore-based family shipping business, says it best: "There's been no conflict in our family historically. We took the avoidance route instead!" He further goes on to explain that one of his and his siblings' priorities is to create a more open family style of family communication:

> I just finished a facilitated dialogue session with my three siblings and two outside consultants. We're in the midst of redefining our values, culture, language, business – we're recreating an identity, which is more sustainable. We need sound discussions to question these fundamentals.

Developing governance structures for the family may be a challenge, particularly in business families with a tradition of powerful leaders or unaddressed conflicts. Unfortunately, the consequences of doing nothing can be serious, as we shall soon see in the story of the Chellaram family. When the founder is no longer there to serve as mediator and the family has not agreed on governance processes to replace his leadership, destructive conflicts can run unchecked.

Kets de Vries and Carlock argue in their 2007 book, *Family Business on the Couch: A Psychological Perspective*, that overcoming relationship conflict requires the ability to supersede individual desires and consider the family's and other stakeholders' collective good. Balancing individual agendas with collective goals is clearly a challenge for many business families, especially when warring siblings appear to be using their family business as a stage to act out their personal rivalries and unresolved grievances. Imagine how powerful such a family business could be if the siblings could start working together instead of competing with each other.

FAMILY GOVERNANCE AS A TOOL FOR CONFLICT PREVENTION AND RESOLUTION

So what can help a business family resolve their relationship conflict? Conflicted families are stuck in a recursive pattern that reinforces destructive interactions as the basis for their relationships. Sham Chellaram, chairman of a Hong Kong shipping and property company, recalls how the business started by his great grandfather experienced conflicts for three generations:

> My grandfather was even more ambitious than his father, so he separated from my great grandfather and expanded overseas. He built a global business with my father and his other sons. But there was conflict once again and my father eventually split the business with his brothers. Our branch prospered and my father passed the baton to my brother and myself. But as the company grew, there was a difference of views of running the business leading to more conflict, so we carved it up yet again.

Chellaram has recognized the value of using governance structures and systems to address family conflicts and build the trust that is essential to breaking the cycle of conflict. He has created both a family and business board that in his words:

> has made the business accountable – and thus has raised the bar to a whole new level. It has made us more conservative, which is a good thing in the shipping business, and more data-driven, which makes us more objective.

Business families find that governance is an effective tool to begin practicing family communication that will help their ongoing family and business relationships.

The cost of avoiding conflict is high. Honest relationships and trust are repressed. The family loses the healthy tension needed for personal growth and change, and it begins to experience the unhealthy kind of tension that stems from limiting individual expression and sharing. Spouses who have heard only complaints from their husbands or wives, and who are often all too willing to take sides, can heighten such tension. Families need to realize that working together and preparing a family and business for the future require uncomfortable changes, mistakes, and confronting conflict.

Organizing family meetings, developing family agreements, and clarifying ownership plans will help prevent unnecessary structural conflicts. Unfortunately, this may not be an adequate solution for the internal strife experienced by some siblings and cousins. When family rivalry or competitiveness becomes the dominant pattern, it may be necessary for senior family members or the family council to resolve the problem. This may mean removing one or more family members from the business, splitting the firm into separate operating companies, creating a holding company, or perhaps even selling the business. Senior family members have a responsibility as stewards of the business to resolve any situation that could result in long-term conflict and destruction of the firm. If they do not take action, the situation will probably never be resolved. In this situation, it is unlikely that the family business will be seen as a desirable opportunity by many members of the next generation.

Constructively confronting each other is a skill that needs to be learned and practiced because it is not typically part of most families' skills or behaviors. Each family needs to think about its particular values and culture as it develops programs to address conflict. Some cultures openly encourage conflict. Family members say what is on their minds with no hesitation. Others discourage addressing disagreements or criticizing another family member.

Either way, the family should have options for conflict resolution spelled out in the family constitution, such as presenting the issue to the family council or to senior family members (sometimes referred to as a council of elders) for a decision. Richard Owens, chairman of R.O.I. Pty Ltd. of Australia, shares his own family's experiences:

> When we started to write our constitution, conflict resolution was right up at the top of the hit parade. It was the most important thing. We did not want to have happen in the next generation what occurred in the previous generation. So there are a couple of pages on conflict resolution, too verbose, but that's the

way we felt at the time. And have we used it? I think we're about to use it. One of the reasons we're pulling out the constitution is to have a look at that.[3]

Alternatively, the issue could be added to the agenda for a family meeting, and the meeting used as a problem-solving session. If the problem is related to a business issue, asking the board of directors to review the situation and suggest a workable resolution is another possibility. It is important to remember that the goal should be to develop a resolution that is acceptable to the disputing parties and compatible with the family's values and vision.

Some families actually invest time in learning conflict resolution skills, rather than depending on mediating mechanisms, such as a family council or board of directors. Others employ a professional to help. They might choose to bring in an expert in organizational development, a trained psychotherapist, or a family business consultant to guide them through a particularly difficult issue.

There is a popular myth that, if something is not talked about, the family relationship will be stronger because there are no fights. However, the reality is that when families have the ability to disagree about important issues – and the tools to resolve their conflict – they develop far more trusting relationships.

FAMILY MEETINGS AS A TOOL FOR PARTICIPATION AND BUILDING TRUST

The starting point for any difficult decision is the family meeting. Family meetings are intended to maintain effective family relationships by improving communications, providing a forum for education, planning, and decision making, and creating accountability. Effective family meetings are the foundation for business families to work together on their shared future. Paddy McNeely, CEO of Meritex, stresses the urgency of adopting this attitude:

We have a lot of opportunity to do things well in the transition from G3 [the third generation] to G4 – and we only just got things right with G3. It's certainly come around fast. The next 10 to 15 years will be crucial. Even if we can get everyone together twice a year, that's only maybe 20 occasions to influence G4's thinking and planning for the future.

Family meetings often develop out of the family's need to clarify its shared aspirations and values. The Malaysian-based Bukit Kiara Group is exploring the family's role by inviting the next generation to form a task force and draft a family charter that "voices your values, what you would like to see in the future, regarding employment, investments, projects, etc." Pauline Tong, a family member and lawyer who is co-leading the effort, goes on to describe perfectly the *Parallel Planning Process*, stating, "We (the family) will meet to discuss how to do certain things which will glue the family together and also do positive things to lead the family business in the same direction as the management team."

Why is something as simple as a meeting so important? First, if the family is unwilling or unable to participate in a meeting, it is a clear signal that its members face challenges in working together. If they cannot agree to hold regular meetings, it is unlikely they will have the skills to work resolve any conflict that might arise. In such cases it might be best to bring in a family business or organizational consultant to get the ball rolling.

Multi-generation families who have never tried meetings before often find it tough to start, simply because of the many different perspectives within the group. But when families make a serious commitment to initiating this process, the meetings generate their own rewards and motivations. Disputes are aired, new ideas surface, and families are often surprised to discover how much potential talent they have in every generation.

Long before formal written agreements are developed or major decisions are taken, these meetings may be used to help educate the family. They may be organized like family "seminars," covering the future leadership skills required and possible family roles. Informal conversation on such subjects can provide a solid foundation for more formal family planning and decision making at a later date.

Agreeing on a family meeting

The mechanics of organizing a family meeting are fairly simple, provided the family works carefully to encourage effective participation. Figure 9.1 identifies a five-step model for organizing a family meeting. As the five steps demonstrate, the overriding goals of the family meeting are: shared participation and planning; discussion and

Figure 9.1 *Preparing effective family meetings*

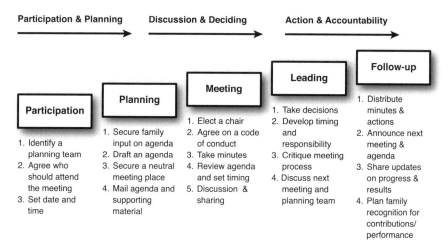

decisions; and action and accountability. There must be an agreement that the meeting will be conducted in a professional manner, with an agenda, chairperson, minutes, and follow-up, otherwise there is a risk of disappointment and frustration.

Preparing a professional and well-planned meeting creates expectations of professional conduct, provides a structure for decision making, and improves outcomes. There are a few critical concerns that all families should consider in developing their family meeting plans:

- Who should attend the meeting?
- How do we develop the agenda?
- Who should lead the meeting?
- What do we discuss at the meeting?
- How do we ensure action and accountability?

Participation: Who should attend family meetings?

Two schools of thought each provide a different answer to this question. One says that only those who are adults and blood relatives should participate. The reasoning here is that sensitive or hurtful family matters should have only a limited audience because it is then easier to maintain confidentiality and prevent emotional injuries. In addition, in-laws or younger members may not fully understand the context. The other perspective maintains that all family members, including teenagers, spouses, and partners should be welcome except in extraordinary situations. These people should be included because the family business affects them and they are important contributors to its success.

Today most family business experts recommend that all family members should attend at least some of the family meetings for the following reasons:

■ In-laws, partners, and children who learn about family plans and issues at first hand have a more realistic picture of the business.
■ Attending meetings helps expose everyone to the family's traditions and processes, and it acquaints them with the family's shared vision and its commitment to the business.
■ The next generation and in-laws can make valuable contributions by providing new perspectives. If the mood of the meeting is right, younger family members may also begin to articulate their own values and intentions regarding the business. Their participation is vital for the family's future and the future of the business.

For many families, the issue of who attends these meetings will settle itself over time. When first holding family meetings, sometimes it is wise to hold a series of "planning sessions" with only the adult, blood family members. This allows the family to establish some ground rules, and saves the embarrassment of exposing in-laws and younger members to a difficult or disorganized meeting that could discourage their long-term participation. One of the outcomes of these pre-meetings is agreement on who attends what meetings and on the role of non-blood relatives.

Planning: How do we develop the agenda?

The way the agenda is crafted sets the tone for the family's participation and contribution. An agenda developed by senior family members leads to a very different meeting than an agenda for which all family members are encouraged to submit ideas. A shared agenda supports effective family communication and allows controversial or sensitive items to surface. The effectiveness of the meeting is not necessarily measured by its content, but rather by how issues are addressed, power is shared, and participation is encouraged. Teams of two or three family members (including the next generation) working together make good task forces to solicit agenda items or issues of mutual interest.

What do we discuss at the family meeting?

The first meeting should center on how the family works together to complete tasks and build stronger social relationships. Many families report that the first real task is to agree on a family code of conduct that structures how they will interact and communicate together in future (see Figure 9.2).

Starting the family's work together by developing a code of conduct has many benefits. First, it reduces conflict through clear rules rather than specific decisions; second, it supports family communication about real issues; and third, it increases effectiveness in achieving a shared vision. The code of conduct also represents the first family agreement, supporting the evolution from reliance on personal trust to reliance on institutional trust.

When a family is just beginning to hold meetings, there are often

Figure 9.2 *Family code of conduct*

Expected Family Behaviors

LISTEN Respectfully with empathy

SPEAK Respectfully

EVERYONE has a voice

Practice Fair Process behaviors and values

Agree on an agenda and critical issues

Breakers of the code earn 10 min with NO voice

Confidentiality must be respected

Do not speak behind other's back

We celebrate shared success

We have fun

too many issues that people want to address. It is helpful to identify just one or two topics that are both important and urgent – and to make decisions and plans of action accordingly. Typically these issues will be related to ownership, careers, or decision making, and will eventually form the basis for formal family agreements. After the family has conducted its first meetings, the agenda will move from legislating agreements and begin to include more planning for family participation and business concerns. The agenda will now include topics related to:

■ planning for ownership development
■ exploring governance structures and nominating directors
■ contributing input to the business strategy
■ ensuring family education and development
■ considering new activities such as philanthropy and other investments.

Who should lead family meetings?

Readers may assume that the natural leader of a family meeting is the business president or a senior family member. Yet such meetings provide the perfect opportunity to broaden the leadership base and give the next generation a chance to practice its leadership and communication skills. With this in mind, the job of organizing and chairing the meeting may best be assigned to a small team from the next generation. Seniors are encouraged to contribute to the planning, but delegating the responsibility is a good opportunity for the next generation to work as a team and to take responsibility for the family's governance.

Sometimes it may be helpful to use a consultant or professional, trained in communication techniques, to facilitate the early family meetings. Some families, for example, bring in a specialist consultant to begin the process and outline the issues. This removes the burden from any one family member, and also encourages questions from the entire group. Whatever the means, the goal is to open up a broad range of topics and enable family members to develop philosophies and agreements that define the family's future relationship with the business – and to strengthen family relationships and the capacity to work together well.

Once the family has successfully completed a few meetings, a family member can be selected to assume the responsibility for chairing and facilitating, supported by a planning task force. It is always possible for a trusted advisor to join the family meeting to address a difficult or technical issue, but the aim should be to develop the family's own capabilities in governance and leadership.

How do we ensure accountability?

Family meetings create expectations. Will the meeting improve family relationships? Will the plans that are enthusiastically discussed during the meeting be implemented? If so, will they lead to changes in behavior and smoother functioning of the family? These are difficult questions because families are not like businesses. To minimize potential frustration it is important that the outcomes of meetings are well documented and communicated to the entire family – first, to ensure agreement and support, and second, to confirm responsibilities and timing for action.

Timely follow-up and reporting create a record of what the family should expect, and also provide checkpoints to monitor performance. Regular updates on projects also help set the stage for the next meeting, which should begin with a report on current projects and results. In many ways, the family meeting or family council serves the same function as a board in ensuring that agreed plans and action are being implemented successfully. Moreover the next family meeting provides an opportunity to revise the plan based on new information and results. It is important to assign projects to a small task force of two or three family members instead of individuals, whenever possible, and to recognize successful performance during subsequent meetings.

FAMILY AGREEMENTS FOR CLARIFYING RIGHTS AND RESPONSIBILITIES

Family agreements are the ground rules that the family needs so that all members can contribute and participate as owners, directors, or employees. They typically address the five generic issues identified in

Chapter 1, as well as any concerns specific to the family, and clarify expected behavior and responsibilities (see Figure 9.3). Family agreements are usually based on family values and represent an ethical rather than legal commitment.

Family agreements can take many forms but, as Adib Al Zamil, managing director of finance and investment for the Zamil Group, Saudi Arabia, points out, "Family constitutions need to be drafted as a precedent before a dispute arises to clarify your actions." There can be many formats ranging from an informal letter to a detailed constitution, signed and ratified by new members as they become adults or marry into the family.

Ideally, family agreements are living documents that evolve over time to reflect changes in the family and business. As Pauline Tong, from the Bukit Kiara Group, says of her own family's new agreement, "It will be a moral agreement amongst us and a continuing working document that can be changed over time to capture changes in reality. It will outline our values, thoughts about family employees, philanthropy, etc."

The *Parallel Planning Process* helps ensure that family agreements are designed to clarify a family's procedures and support the business' needs. Family agreements tend to reduce conflict if:

Figure 9.3 *Family agreements addressing the five generic challenges of business families*

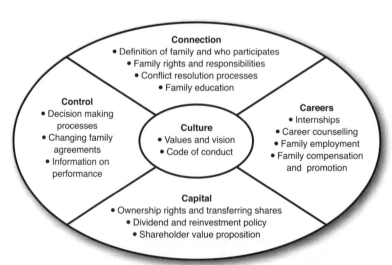

- they are based on consensus
- they are communicated to all members
- they are applied consistently
- there is a mechanism for modifying the agreement based on changing conditions.

Typical family agreement topics

Often the first family agreement is about succession and the next generation joining the family business. Luay Abu-Ghazaleh, vice chairman of Talal Abu-Ghazaleh Organization, a leading professional services group based in the Middle East, describes his family's experience:

> The succession plan has developed into what we call, ironically for a Moslem family, our "family bible". It is now much more than a succession plan. It sets out the rules for joining the firm. But it is not set in stone. We change it as we go along. My father wanted us all to agree not to be dictated to.

We will use careers to demonstrate the thinking that is needed to draft a family agreement. As we saw in Chapter 1, family employment has the potential to create conflict because of parents' natural desire to support their children's careers, and their psychological tendency to see their children's accomplishment as a reflection of themselves. An agreement about family employment should be treated just like any other written contract. If the rules change, everyone needs to be told why as well as how. Individual members should also understand what the new rules mean to them. Surprise or betrayal in this regard may undermine trust in the entire family enterprise. Typical employment questions that need to be answered in a family employment agreement are shown in Figure 9.4. It is important to note that employment in the company impacts on the family, so the family needs to work closely with management to ensure that the family's wishes are aligned with the strategy developed by the management team.

Compensation and promotions

Several approaches are available based on the family's philosophy and on the business itself. One approach is that standard business practices

Figure 9.4 *Family agreement questions*

Employment agreements

When and under what circumstances can family members join the business?

Do they fill a vacant post or is one created for them?

What education and previous work experience do they need?

At what age is it no longer possible to join the firm? At age 30 or maybe 40? Should there be a limit at all?

Can a family member re-enter the family business after a voluntary or involuntary departure? Scenarios in this case would include leaving for child rearing, graduate school, or a serious work issue that resulted in a termination of employment.

How are internships and part-time work handled?

Are in-laws welcome to join the company and, if so, in what capacities?

---

will apply. That is, salaries are based on market and performance criteria, and the business must always come first. However, while competitive salary scales encourage good performance, they may also produce family conflicts.

A second approach puts the family first. All family members' incomes are equal. All difficult decisions are made by consensus. The "president" may actually be a team of family members, whose job is to see that consensus is reached rather than to make tough decisions. The risk here is that business performance is sacrificed for the sake of family harmony.

Either way, the management should consider the benefits of openly publicizing compensation levels among all family members. This minimizes the likelihood of anyone drawing incorrect conclusions based on lifestyles or assumptions. It also sends out a clear signal that family members depend on one another for their mutual success – financial and otherwise.

Assign positions based on business needs

Until one of them is named president, next-generation family members should not be required to report to each other, if at all possible. Each should also have his or her own niche within the company, from a special project to managing a full division. If members of the next generation perform well and are rewarded for their efforts, they will feel that they are making valuable contributions to the business. This softens the sting of watching one sibling gain a higher title. Eventually too, separate career paths may pave the way for corporate spin-offs or new ventures with new leadership possibilities.

Family behavior in the business

The behavior of family members towards employees or other stake-holders (such as customers or suppliers) requires exemplary conduct. Family conduct can even have serious legal and public relations consequences for the business. And if family members do not treat other employees properly, the morale of the entire company can be threatened. In short, poor individual behavior can send a very negative signal to employees and other stakeholders about the family's values and ability to lead.

Employment and the family's code of conduct

Employment in the family firm creates an expectation that family members will act in a manner conducive to the business' reputation. Those who argue constantly with one another, confront each other in the workplace, or make disrespectful remarks about one another in public, are undermining the family's commitment to a shared vision for the business. Often the code of conduct will need to be expanded to include rules on how family members work together and with other stakeholders (see Figure 9.5).

THE FAMILY COUNCIL – PROFESSIONALIZING FAMILY GOVERNANCE

As the family grows in size and complexity (numbers, geography, branches, multiple generations, and so on), regular family meetings may need to be replaced by a smaller but representative family council. The full family meeting often continues as an annual family assembly that provides the family with a chance to socialize, share concerns, and ratify the actions of the smaller group on the family council.

Typically the transition to a family council represents a need for a

Figure 9.5 *Family employee code of conduct*

Employment Code of Conduct

We will support each other and the family

We will share recognition

We will act according to the family's values

We will respect each other's professionalism

We will not exploit any business opportunities for personal gain

We will not expose the business to legal or public relations problems

We will conduct relationships with employees ethically.

more professional approach to addressing family issues and to interacting with the business and board, as part of the *Parallel Planning Process*. Sophie Lammerant-Velge, a family council member, explains why her Belgian family made the decision to organize a family council:

> Bekaert is a listed company with 23,000 employees in 120 countries. The family is now very large, with members representing the third to the sixth generation. There are eight family members on the Bekaert board and fourteen on the Family Council. The role of the Family Council is to solve all family matters before they reach the board, which has to concentrate on strategic and business issues. It's important that the family speaks with a single voice.

The creation of a family council is a logical step that complements the business governance provided by the board of directors. It marks a new phase of family governance that is more strategic and driven by planning. The family council assumes a more proactive role in identifying required family actions and engaging with the board of directors (see Figure 9.6).

Family decisions on creating a family council

Families that plan to form a family council should consider the responsibilities of the council in relation to the business and its model of

Figure 9.6 *Family council responsibilities*

Family council actions

Developing family education plans

Ensuring accountability for the implementation of plans

Interacting with the board member selection

Reviewing family values and vision

Organizing family and shareholder meetings

Encouraging participation in family activities

Developing family leaders from the next generation

Developing family social and philanthropic activities.

---

family representation. If the council evolves from a tradition of family meetings, then the family will have accepted the idea of shared planning and decision making. Family members will have experienced the value of working together to arrive at an understanding about critical issues. Any concerns about the council's decision-making authority can be addressed by providing a ratification procedure at the annual family assembly.

A multi-generational family or one with a large number of members may also benefit from the representational approach that widens participation. Younger family members, those who are not employed by the business, or those who are not currently shareholders, may find that a representative family council is more open to hearing their ideas and addressing their concerns. The nomination or election of family council members also creates leadership opportunities for a more diverse group of family members.

The hard part is deciding how to select a representative group to serve on the council, especially if family meetings have traditionally been organized and led by the senior generation. Some families may want to ensure representation from different branches, or a balance between members employed by the business and those working elsewhere. Others will try to maintain a balance between different generations. Some very successful families avoid the problem altogether by seeking the best candidates, regardless of family branch, generation, or job. Some also find success with a rotational method of participation.

The family council and social activities

Perpetuating a successful business family should not be all work. All families should spend some social time together. And the family council often takes responsibility for planning social activities. Enjoying social or recreational activities together builds rapport, friendship, and ease of communication among family members. It is best to leave business concerns totally out of these occasions, thus helping to create effective boundaries between the family and business. Family members, particularly those who are not employed by the firm, can feel that they are not on equal footing or a full member of the family, if there is constant reference to business.

Many families "formalize fun" through regular vacations or by purchasing a farm, summer cottage, or resort condominium for shared use. Some families include a formal statement in their family agreements that family holidays, vacations, and religious celebrations, will be exclusively centered on family experiences and will not include discussions of the business or its issues.

FAMILY SHAREHOLDER AGREEMENTS

Entrepreneurs and business families approach ownership planning in many different ways. Often entrepreneurs take an "It's not 'when' but 'if' I'm going to die" attitude, and make no provision for distribution of assets or control after their death. Many business families avoid conversations about inheritance for fear of the conflicts and emotions that such discussions may unleash. Either way, there is potential for long-drawn-out legal battles that never result in improved business performance or family harmony.

Consider the case of Formosa Plastics and its founder Wang Yung-Ching, who died without a will last year in the United States. Wang, who was Taiwan's second-richest man, died at age 91 leaving control of his global business empire uncertain. A New Jersey judge has refused to dismiss a lawsuit started by his son over who should administer the multi-billion-dollar estate and whether it should be decided under US or Taiwanese laws. The case is currently pending and will involve many years of legal hearings before the assets can finally be distributed among the heirs.

An opposite approach that supports the goals of the *Parallel Planning Process* is to plan actively for ownership continuity. Luay Abu-Ghazaleh of Talal Abu-Ghazaleh Organization describes how his father recognized the need for succession planning early on:

> My father's vision comes less from textbooks and business school teaching than from his own professional experience. Ours is a professional services firm, so he has seen things go sour in many, many family businesses. When we were still young enough not to have developed "agendas" of our own, he got us all together – my mother, my brother, my two sisters, and I – to talk about what would happen when he died. We all got upset and my mother was angry. We didn't discuss it. On his third attempt, he sent us full documentation (a couple of hundred pages) in advance, arranged the meeting in Paris, and made sure his lawyers were there. We didn't have any choice but to discuss succession.

Creating estate plans is one of the toughest projects for the senior generation because it means addressing very sensitive issues. This is never an easy conversation, because it hits all of the social taboos and sensitivities, including parental control, autonomy, death, respect, love, lifestyle, in-laws and partners, divorce, gender, and children. It often requires planning and action at the individual, branch, and whole-family levels.

On an individual basis, each person must face his or her own mortality and then consider how financial assets will be distributed to others. In some cases estate planning involves each branch of the family to maintain overall ownership balance. Action may also be required by the whole family if there are trusts, voting agreements, or buy–sell plans in place. These structures are important because family businesses must balance the needs of the different generations and ensure that the business remains financially viable and competitive.

Shareholder agreements are legal contracts that serve three important purposes. First, they provide a framework for defining ownership rights and responsibilities. Second, they create a framework for resolving disputes or conflicts over ownership. (Note that many families include ownership in their family agreements, which are typically more ethically than legally binding. It is important to caution that all actions related to ownership must be carefully considered in the light of expert legal and tax advice.) Third and equally important, ownership agreements shape the ownership structure to support the family's vision of the business and itself. Just as it is important to develop employment and work-related family agreements before the next generation joins the firm, so it is vital to develop agreements on a wide range of ownership matters before shares are promised or transferred.

Another purpose of ownership agreements is to clarify shareholder rights. Unfortunately, rights in privately held companies are more dependent on relationships and clear understandings than on corporate charters, laws, or government regulations. Shareholders in public companies have well-defined rights because stock markets, government agencies, and courts set minimum standards and enforce regulations related to shareholder meetings, disclosure of financial information, boards of directors, voting rights, and other business issues. These are tools that are seldom utilized by business families except in extreme cases –as demonstrated by the McNeely case study earlier in this chapter.

If the family has agreed to a vision that includes continuity of family ownership, then ownership planning and transition is a critical topic – not an easy one, but there still needs to be agreement about where the family wants to be in the future. As in all other aspects of family business planning, life cycles are a key factor. As discussed in the previous chapter, ownership is based on the current owner's intentions. If a senior family member owns shares of stock, it is his or hers to do with as he or she chooses, unless there are religious, buy–sell, or other legal restrictions. Ownership also represents the senior generation's life style and economic security, as well as funds for philanthropy and assets to share with heirs. This may include distributing some of the parents' assets to children who have decided not to participate in the family business.

Conflict often occurs when shareholders want to sell but are locked into ownership. This can be particularly complex if one of the shareholders has an unexpected personal or business financial need and there is no other way to get at the cash. A liquidity plan, often known as a buy–sell agreement or redemption policy, allows family members to sell stock either because they want to invest elsewhere or because they simply do not want to own a part of the family business any more. Whatever the case, it is important for the family to have an efficient and easy way to administer a program to redeem, redistribute, or transfer family stock so that the business is protected and family relationships maintained.

In a privately controlled family business it is often impractical to depend on outside intervention to enforce ownership rights. A family that manages its affairs based on strict interpretation of legal requirements or the threat of legal action loses its natural competitive advantage of trust. What many families find useful is to develop family ownership agreements that articulate the family's understandings about what it means to be a shareholder in the family.

Facilitating discussion of these uncertainties, of course, is what the *Parallel Planning Process* is supposed to do. It is meant to encourage honest exchanges and full disclosure of both family and business concerns. The only way to resolve the challenges of ownership is for the family to discuss the financial positions of the business and the family openly. In some families, estate planning brings to the surface some unresolved issues, such as who wants to accept the responsibilities of business ownership. In such cases, the family must resolve the issues before the company can be sure that its business strategies are appropriate.

FROM FAMILY BUSINESSES TO FAMILY OFFICES AND FOUNDATIONS

Families that have sold their business or created substantial wealth often create family offices and foundations as vehicles to manage their assets and their charitable giving. The two structures serve different purposes: the family office exists primarily to provide investment and financial planning, tax, accounting, and some family services, while the foundation is designed to support a more strategic or unified approach to family philanthropy.

Just as in the original business, family values and vision can provide a competitive advantage for investment. James Chen, head of Legacy Advisors, Ltd, his family's family office in Hong Kong, observes that "In a crisis, particularly, you need a single vision. That's what we had through the recent economic upheaval. There was no temptation to panic, to go to cash. And we're already back up to our peak net asset value."

Likewise, a successful foundation will turn the family's values into highly effective philanthropic action and – if part of a truly *Parallel Planning Process* – link back into the business. Shannon McNeely Whitaker, sister of Meritex CEO Paddy, and daughter of Harry Jr. (with whose story we began this chapter) has never worked for the business but is chair of the family foundation. She explains:

> The business and foundation are "sister" enterprises – part of the same community. The foundation has gone back to our family roots and focuses on its philanthropy in the neighborhood where my grandfather founded the business. It supports and encourages employee giving in all corporate locations and communities through an employee gift-matching program. The Foundation also offers a scholarship program for employees' children attending college.

Above all, however, these two structures often serve to replace the business in holding the family together. The case of the McNeelys may be an extreme example of a family rift healed through a Cousin Collaboration foundation. But a strong family office, linked to a foundation, can prevent a rift from occurring in the first place. Roy Chen, who oversees investment operations for his family's office, Grace Financial Ltd in Hong Kong, strongly endorses this idea:

> Giving is implicit in the idea of stewardship. And if you give, by definition you have to look beyond yourself. I think it's well proven that the most effective glue beyond the third generation is philanthropy. Investment can be daunting for the next generation to get involved with, but something like the long-term eradication of hepatitis B is something that the whole family has rallied around. Philanthropy isn't an option. It's a necessity.

WHEN FAMILY BUSINESSES ARE BEST

- Family meetings or councils provide governance processes to support communication and decision-making for the family.
- Family agreements clearly describe family behavior and rules for working together on critical topics.
- Shareholder agreements protect the family's assets from disputes and allow long-term planning and actions.
- The family foundation and family office are tools for maintaining family connection and commitment beyond the operating business.

Part V

Family Enterprise Stewardship

10 The Men and Women Who Plant Trees

Exactly a century ago on the bare contours of the southern French Alps, one man began to plant trees.

Elzéard Bouffier had been a farmer in the lowlands, but – after the death of his wife and only son – he withdrew to the mountains with his sheep. However, it was not his intention to live out his last years as a shepherd, alone on the arid slopes scattered with long-abandoned villages. He had a simple purpose: to bring the withered landscape back to life by populating it with trees.

Bouffier spent his days planting acorns and his evenings sorting through the next batch of seeds, selecting only the best. He also started to introduce other species, such as beech and birch. Over three years, he planted 100,000 seeds in total. Of these, only one-fifth produced seedlings. And he knew that only half of these again would survive. But that would still leave 10,000 trees – growing in a place where once there had been nothing.

The years went by, and with them the Great War. Elzéard Bouffier continued his single-minded pursuit. By now the first oaks were as tall as a man, and the beech trees shoulder high. In the valleys birch thickets were thriving, and water ran in the beds of streams that had been dry throughout living memory. Meanwhile, Bouffier had sold all but four of his sheep, as the flock had begun to eat too many seedlings and to drink too much of the water, the scarcest resource of all. Instead he acquired a hundred beehives, from which he was able to earn a basic living.

Little by little, as the years went by, wildlife returned to the landscape: first flowers and willow trees, then hare and wild boar. Hunters followed in their tracks, but no one yet suspected that man, let alone one single man, was responsible for this apparent miracle of nature. And still Bouffier continued – with no recognition, yet much adversity. One year he planted more than 10,000 maples, all of which died. But the rest of the forest flourished to the point that he now had to walk 12 km from his house to plant new beech trees. Bouffier was 75 years old and had almost forgotten how to talk, such was his solitary lifestyle.

When the Second World War broke out, his work was briefly in jeopardy. Some of the trees were cut down for much-needed fuel, but the forest was so remote that it soon became apparent that felling them was uneconomical. Bouffier continued planting, just as he had through the First World War. By the time a distant peace was declared in 1945, he was 87. He died in hospital two years later.

During the last years of the old man's life, a wise forestry officer had come to realize that the trees had not sprung up spontaneously. He had, unbeknown to Bouffier, assigned some of his staff to protect the young forest. At around the same time, families had begun to return to the abandoned farms and villages. Water became plentiful, as the trees retained the snow and the people learned how to channel streams. Crops of all kinds grew abundantly.

Elzéard Bouffier left behind him not only a forest of thousands of trees but a community of nearly 10,000 men, women, and children. His once-bleak mountainside lived happily – if not ever after – right up to the present day.

FROM PLANTING TO PLANNING

"The man who planted trees" is clearly *not* a story about family business. Its original author, the French writer, Jean Giono, was never even clear as to whether it was fact or fiction. He claimed instead that it was a modern fable. Indeed, since he first published it back in 1954 the short story has been translated into all major languages and turned into a Oscar-winning animated film in 1987.[1]

No doubt the fable is more relevant than ever in an age where planting trees could quite literally save our planet. But for us, it is above all a story that sums up all that is – or can be – best about family business. Perhaps too, just as business families can learn from the man who planted trees, so other companies can learn from the example set by family firms.

Ultimately, "The man who planted trees" is about an ordinary human being who channels his creativity and energy into a vision and accomplishes extraordinary things. His values of focusing on the future, continuous learning, and working strategically, combined with the entrepreneurial determination to do something that had never been done before, enabled him to transform the arid countryside into a thriving landscape filled with wildlife and happy, prospering families. Without any thought of personal recognition or gain, the shepherd turned forester moved telessly across the countryside, selecting and planting the best trees for the different soil and landscapes. In short, this it is a story about the outcome of sound planning – what we call *stewardship*.

Jean Giono's story also returns us to the starting point of this book – values and vision – and enables us to close it by insisting on the importance of the human dimension of family business. As business professors, it is easy for us to suggest new thinking about strategy, investment, and governance. These are technical topics where we can offer relevant information based on our research, teaching, and advisory experience. Yet, in reality, the most important factors in working with business families are their values and vision. If the family's motivations do not support a commitment to working together to build a long-lasting business, then our ideas about planning are of little practical value.

In this chapter we do something that we have attempted to avoid throughout the book. We are going to make a specific recommendation that you consider including stewardship as an overriding value for your family and business. When we say family and business "stewardship," we literally mean how you raise your children, how you lead the business, and the type of legacy your family aspires to. Wealthy and successful families face a difficult challenge, because maintaining their family connections or glue is not easy. This is where stewardship can play a role in helping create shared meaning in their lives. A strong set of values can hold a business family together, and more importantly, offset the natural tendency for wealth and power to interfere with normal human relationships.

We know that many of you have stewardship or continuity or perpetuity in some form as a family value, but we believe that there is a particularly complementary relationship between stewardship and the *Parallel Planning Process*. Stewardship is the value, and the *Parallel Planning Process* activities of visioning, strategizing, investing and governing are the behaviors, that build legacies of success for family businesses. Family business stewardship can take many different forms:

- using family values as the basis for planning and actions
- teaching your children about the responsibilities of wealth
- funding family education and talent development
- ensuring the business has the resources to grow
- selecting the most capable management team available
- planning for ownership transitions
- continually monitoring business opportunities and threats
- preparing the family and business for change
- developing programs to support family participation and commitment
- contributing family talents and resources to philanthropy
- developing sound family agreements to prevent conflicts
- using governance to take decisions and improve accountability
- practicing fair process in all family and business dealings
- protecting the interests of the communities served by the family business.

The best families consciously work at stewardship, because passing on a better business than inherited or founded to children and grand-children is of high purpose. A healthy business with sound prospects provides options for future generations and builds a legacy based on family values, participation, and a commitment to creating value for all stakeholders.

Most businesses, just like the forest in the story of Elzéard Bouffier, simply do not grow naturally. Then they last one or two generations and simply fade away. Dr. Léon Danco, one of the early consultants to study family business, first observed this phenomenon 30 years ago. His thinking challenged business families to professionalize their planning. He lamented that the lack of effective planning by family, owners and managers was a leading cause of business failure. Danco's challenge to the field of family business influenced our previous books: *Keeping the Family Business Healthy* by John Ward, *Strategic Planning for the Family Business,* which we co-authored, and now *When Family Businesses Are Best*.

We believe that business families achieve their potential when the owners and leaders develop effective family and business plans supported by stewardship values. Stewardship alone is just a good intention – it requires a constructive framework like the *Parallel*

Planning Process to help members of the family team understand their roles and take decisions and actions that support the business' future success. The five steps of the *Parallel Planning Process* are the tools that transform stewardship from an idea into a professional behavior. While our book is written for business families, we believe that it offers a planning template for the twenty-first century. As the global environment becomes more threatening and businesses become more complex, we doubt that many organizations, either family or widely traded, will grow without sound planning and a longer-term, stewardship-driven approach.

The results of planning for a family business are not, of course, predetermined. For most readers, this book presumes, planning – especially the *Parallel Planning Process* – will sharpen the choice of strategy and strengthen the family's commitment to the business. If so, the increased reinvestment by the owners will enhance the business strategy's chances for success and the family business' long-term continuity. For some families, the *Parallel Planning Process* will lead to a different, but perhaps equally appropriate, result. They may accept more conclusively and comfortably that business continuity is not the best goal for them.

For other families, the *Parallel Planning Process* will help them realize that potential exists and that commitment is for some family members, but not all. They may choose to strengthen commitment by providing ownership redemption opportunities for those less interested. Coming to that conclusion pro-actively and gracefully strengthens the chances for both business success and family harmony. If owners and leaders act as stewards and if the family feels that processes are fair, the full potential and benefit of the family business' strengths are realized. Families that respect both stewardship and *Fair Process* will find the *Parallel Planning Process* an invaluable tool and worthwhile adventure.

STEWARDSHIP AS THE REAL MEASURE OF FAMILY BUSINESS PERFORMANCE

Typically, business performance is measured on two metrics: operating results and value creation (see Figure 10.1). Operating performance is a financial measure of efficiency taking into account the business' results over recent periods in terms of cash flow, productivity, and profitability. These are the key criteria of the health of a business, and both the management and the board will monitor them on a quarterly and annual basis.

The second metric, value creation, measures the effectiveness of the business' strategy and the management's execution in creating long-term value for shareholders and all stakeholders. Criteria include new market development, sound financials, the quality of the management team, and effective governance. These are important indicators of the business' longer-term health and ability to create future value.

Family businesses have a third measure of performance, which we label "stewardship." It is not a measure of the business' outputs, but rather assesses the family's ongoing contribution – as owners and leaders – to its own success and that of the business. Stewardship measures the family's efforts in terms of its human and financial investment, leadership, and governance behavior, and most important, the way in which it enacts values like professionalism, concern for employees, philanthropy, or fairness. Business families require an expanded set of performance metrics because their success is not simply measured by financial performance. Families, as discussed in Chapter 1, often expect social, psychological, and spiritual returns on their investment.

Figure 10.1 *Three measures of family business performance*

Metric & Timing	Performance Measures
Stewardship 5 to 20 years	Family investment Family leadership Family governance Family philanthropy
Value Creation 2 to 5 years	Capable management Business governance Financial strength New market growth
Operating 1 to 2 years	Profit margin Sales growth Cash flow Productivity

THE COMPETITIVE ADVANTAGE OF STEWARDSHIP

Stewardship is a potential competitive advantage for all business families – provided they plan and govern to exploit it. Effective planning artfully capitalizes on every possible family business strength or advantage. Although it is impossible to list all of the unique advantages of family businesses, there are natural strengths that the best family firms often possess by the very nature of the fact that they are family controlled. It is interesting that many of these strengths are demonstrated in "The man who planted trees."

The following section reviews the five steps of our *Parallel Planning Process* and how they can turn natural family business strengths into competitive advantages.

Family values mean something

Widely traded companies must often set their standards of excellence through costly and time-consuming personnel and management controls. But family companies are driven by shared values and a sense of pride in their people, products, or services. It is their name above the door. Elzéard Bouffier valued quality as a driving force in his work, and was inherently motivated to do things right. Family firms tend to value quality too. They often respond to customer complaints more quickly than larger or more widely held companies. Family companies take such complaints personally since they come from neighbors. For customers large and small, a family business can provide that "personal touch" so important in today's frequently impersonal business world.

Family visions are in generations

The story of Elzéard Bouffier also demonstrates how focusing a vision on the long term can get results. His vision of creating a forest – where before there was nothing – supported a simple strategy of planting 100,000 trees over three years, knowing that only 20,000 would result in seedlings and that just half of those would survive to form a forest in several decades' time. He followed his dream, even though he knew he would not be there to see it become a full reality. The best family businesses are in for the long haul too. They are able to look beyond the results for the quarter or even the year, to the next generation and beyond.

Families plan for new opportunities

Niche or specialty markets often provide greater opportunities than larger, mass markets because there are fewer players – and that means more profit to go around. The company that first makes a name for itself in such a market can usually create a barrier to other competitors.

Family businesses are eminently suited to taking advantage of such market opportunities. They do not have to answer to shareholders and investment professionals. Instead, with the right family commitment, they have the freedom to experiment with new markets and opportunities – even if they have to wait one or two decades for the eventual payoff.

This was also the case for Elzéard Bouffier. As sheep no longer became his central concern and in fact began to threaten his main enterprise of nurturing a forest, he turned instead to bees for his livelihood. He practiced perfect stewardship of scarce resources like water and young birch trees. He knew his values and what was right, and so he never gave up on his vision – but as he aged and his environment evolved, he planned and adapted to take advantage of new opportunities.

Families invest for the next generation

One of the oldest clichés about business is particularly true for family businesses: Successful businesses are successful because they invest for the future. And the best family businesses are the best because they invest their talent and resources in developing their human capital and capabilities as owners and leaders. Similarly, Elzéard Bouffier was continually learning. He knew far more about trees than the forestry official who one day came along and warned him not to light fires, as it might endanger the "natural forest."

The best family businesses offer training programs, family seminars, coaching, time off for professional or industry associations, even funding for further formal education. Family companies can gain high returns from such investments because they result in long-term loyalty and commitment. A family company that develops, promotes, and rewards based on contribution to the family, benefits from the commitment of the entire family whose interest it has encouraged. A family leader who has no interest in business matters becomes a committed owner when a son or daughter works for the family business or chooses to support it in other ways. Like Elzéard Bouffier, he or she is not yet ready to withdraw from life while working for the benefit of the next generations.

Families govern for performance

A universal challenge facing family businesses is the inherent conflicts that exist between the values and thinking of families and businesses. These two powerful systems – when aligned in their vision and planning – create outstanding value for their stakeholders, but this requires sound governance based on effective decision making and accountability. The well-governed family business that plans in parallel for itself and its business, based on a shared vision, can react more quickly to new opportunities. It can do this because a few people make these decisions, not a slow-moving corporate bureaucracy. Just before Elzéard Bouffier died, the forester with foresight did exactly what was needed. That is, nothing at all – except for guaranteeing that the forest would be placed under the protection of the state and that all commercial felling of the trees would be strictly prevented. In the same way, effective governance processes prevent conflict and protect family relationships without undue interference.

FAMILIES CREATE SHARED SUCCESS

"The man who planted trees" is a parable about stewardship: an ordinary man who had no need for recognition or power toiled persistently without expectation of personal gain. The work and his ability to contribute to the future was his reward.

The social glue created by shared success may be the most important reason for family business ownership. Members of the best business families create opportunities to recognize each other's contributions, to show appreciation for efforts, and to develop pride in accomplishments that non-business families seldom get to experience. It is only when families work together that father, mother, daughter, son, uncle, aunt, sister, brother, or cousin see one another in leadership roles, serving others and the family itself.

Family businesses create a special place where their families can share and enjoy their successes and support each other during setbacks. These shared experiences – if supported by clear boundaries, such as family agreements, and sound structures, like boards and family councils – form strong bonds. In such a close-knit environment, family members share the big achievements but also the small, often unrecognized, contributions, which are not even expected. These hidden successes are reinforced in a thousand ways, from a kind word by a senior relative, a smile from an employee after an important decision, the laughter of children at a community event, or the feeling that comes from helping a struggling family member achieve something positive in their life.

This is when family businesses are best.

Notes

Preface

1   Kets de Vries, M. and Carlock, R. S. with Florent-Treacy, E. *Family Business on the Couch: A Psychological Perspective*, (New York: John Wiley and Sons, 2007).

1 Why Family Businesses Struggle

1   Anderson, R. and Reeb, D. "Founding family ownership and firm performance: Evidence from the S&P 500," *Journal of Finance* 58, 2003, and "Dynasty and durability," *Economist*, September 7, 2009.

2   Carlock, R.S. "Farview Electronics to be sold?" (unpublished INSEAD case study, 2010).

3   Freud, S. *Civilization and its Discontents*, (London: Hogarth Press, 1955).

4   Making a Difference (2007–08) PricewaterhouseCoopers Family Business Services.

5   "Dynasty and durability," *Economist*, September 7, 2009.

6   Gersick, K. E., Davis, J. A., McCollom Hampton, M., and Lansberg, I. *Generation to Generation: Life Cycles of the Family Business* (Boston, Mass.: Harvard Business School Press, 1997).

7   Erikson, E. H. *Childhood and Society* (New York: W.W. Norton, 1950).

8   "Dynasty and durability," *Economist*, September 7, 2009.

9   Adapted from Sigelman, C. K. and Shaffer, D. R. *Life-Span Development,* (Belmont, Calif.: Brooks/Cole, 1991); Eggers, J. H., Leahy, K. T., and Churchill, N. C. *The Seasons of a Man's Life*, New York: Balantine Books, 1978); "Stages of small business growth revisited: Insights into growth path and leadership/management skills in low and high growth companies," in Bygrave, W. D., Birely, S., Churchill, N. C., Gatewood, E., Hoy, F., and Wetzel, W. E. (eds), *Frontiers of Entrepreneurship Research* (Boston, Mass.,: Babson College, 1994).

10   Handler, W. C. "Succession experiences of the next generation," *Family Business Review*, 1992.

11 Making a Difference (2007–08), PricewaterhouseCoopers Family Business Services.
12 Information for this case is taken from several sources: "Family dynamics: Why Bancrofts shifted stance on the Dow Jones bid," *Wall Street Journal*, June 12, 2007; "Prelude to a meeting," *Wall Street Journal*, June 4, 2007; "Bancroft cousin's letter: 'Paying the price for our passivity,'" *Wall Street Journal*, July 27, 2007; "How Thomson recast itself for a new era," *Wall Street Journal*, June 12, 2007; and Carlock, R. S., Kets de Vries, M., and Florent-Treacy, E. "Family matters: Keeping it in the family," *World Business Magazine* (December 2007).
13 "Bancroft cousin's letter: 'paying the price for our passivity,'" *Wall Street Journal*, July 27, 2007.

2 Making the Parallel Family and Business Planning Process Work

1 Broehl, W. G. *Cargill: Trading the World's Grain* (Hanover, N.H.: University Press of New England, 1992).
2 "Cargill faces future with a new face," Reuters, May 18, 2007.
3 Kampmeyer, J. M. "Preparing the next generation of owners (at Cargill)," Kellogg School of Management Family Business Conference, May 16–17, 2006.
4 Carlock, R. "Cheers to French entrepreneurs," *Families-in-Business*, November 21, 2008.
5 "Fellow travelers" in English, meaning employees and stakeholders who support them.

3 Family Values and Business Culture

1 Schein, E. H. "The role of the founder in creating organizational culture," *Organizational Dynamics*, 12 (1983).
2 Carlock, R. S. *Eu Yan Sang: Healing a Family and Business* (INSEAD case study, 2004).
3 Ward, J. L. and Zsolnay, C. A. *Murugappa Group: Centuries-Old Business Heritage and Tradition,* (Kellogg School of Management case study, 2004).
4 Ward, J. L. and Zsolnay, C. A. *Succession and Continuity for Johnson Family Enterprises (A),* (Kellogg School of Management case study, 2004),
5 Ward, J. L. and Lief, C. *Prudence and Audacity: The House of Beretta* (IMD case study, 2005).
6 Abdon, E., Engellau, E., Florent-Treacy, E., Guillen, L., and Marmenout, K. under the supervision of Kets de Vries. M. *Fatima Al Jaber and Al Jaber Group: Traditions and transitions in a United Arab Emirates Family Enterprise* (INSEAD case study, 2009).

7   Watson, N. and Story, J. *MAS Holdings: Strategic Corporate Social Responsibility – A Strategy for the Apparel Industry* (INSEAD case study, 2005).
8   Van der Heyden, L., Blondel, C., and Carlock, R. "Fair Process: striving for justice in family firms," *Family Business Review* (March, 2005).
9   Kim, W. C. and Mauborgne, R. "Fair Process: managing in the knowledge economy," *Harvard Business Review*, 75 (July–August 1997).
10 Kenyon-Rouvinez, D. *Sharing Wisdom, Building Values* (Marietta, Ga: Family Enterprise Publishers, 2002).
11 Collins, J. C. and Lazier, W. C. *Beyond Entrepreneurship* (New York: Prentice Hall, 1992).

4 Family Business Vision: Exploring Family Commitment

1   Collins, J. C. and Porras, J. L. *Built to Last: Successful Habits of Visionary Companies* (New York: HarperBusiness, 1994).
2   Mowday, R. T., Steers R. M., and Porter, L. W. "The measurement of organizational commitment," *Journal of Vocational Behavior* 14 (1979).
3   Carlock, R. A. "Classroom discussion with James R. Cargill," *Family Business Review* (Fall 1994).
4   Carlock, R. S. *Eu Yan Sang: Healing a Family and Business* (INSEAD case study, 2006).

5 Family Participation: Planning the Family's Future

1   Larsen, P. T. "Blueprint for keeping business in the family – interview with Andrew Wates," *Financial Times,* July 25, 2007.
2   Senge, P. M. *The Fifth Discipline: The Art and Practice of the Learning Organization*, (New York: Doubleday Currency, 1990).
3   Johnson, L. "Poor children of the rich and famous," *Financial Times*, May 6, 2009.
4   The term "senior-generation leadership" refers to an individual or group of family members, such as the CEO or the owners, who currently have ultimate control of the family firm. The next generation is the individual or team of family members that will control the family firm through leadership or ownership in the future.
5   Florent, E. *Work and Love: Finding One's Place in the Family Firm* (INSEAD case study 10/2002-5005, 2002-5).
6   Levinson, H. "Why the behemoths fell: Psychological roots of corporate failure," *American Psychologist*, 1994.
7   Kets de Vries, M. F. R. *Family Business: Human Dilemmas in the Family Firm* (London: International Thomson Business Press, 1996).

8   Kets de Vries, M. and Carlock, R. S. with Florent-Treacy, E. *Family Business on the Couch: A Psychological Perspective* (New York: John Wiley, 2007).
9   Davis, J. and Tagiuri, R. "Bivalent attributes of the family firm," *Family Business Review* (1996).
10 Timberlake, C. "The ladder–Oedipus complex: How to get help for a family business," *Wall Street Journal Europe*, February 27, 2001.
11 Herz Brown, F. "Parenting, privilege and challenging tomorrow's leaders," *Families in Business* (2004).

6 Business Strategy: Planning the Firm's Future

1   Source: Carlock, Randel S. "Family psychology and competitive advantage," *Families in Business*, July 21, 2008.
2   Drucker, P. "The future has already happened," *Harvard Business Review,* 1997.
3   Levitt, T. "Marketing myopia," *Harvard Business Review*, September–October, 1975.
4   Porter, M. "What is strategy?" *Harvard Business Review*, November–December 1996.
5   Porter, M. *Competitive Strategy* (New York: Free Press, 1980).

7 Investing for Family Business Success

1   Villalonga, B. and Amit, R. "How do family ownership, control, and management affect firm value?" *Journal of Financial Economics*, May 2006.
2   Ugo Gussalli Beretta quoted in Wilson, R. L. *The World of Beretta: An International Legend* (New York: Random House, 2000).
3   Adapted from De Visscher, F., Aronoff, C. and Ward J. *Financing Transitions: Managing Capital and Liquidity in Family Businesses* (Marietta, Ga.: Business Owners Resources, 1995).
4   Kaye, K. "When family business is a sickness," *Family Business Review* (1996).
5   "Prelude to a Murdoch meeting," *Wall Street Journal,* June 4, 2007.

8 Family Business Governance and the Role of the Board of Directors

1   Carlock, R. S. and Florent-Treacy, E. *Nash Engineering: 100 years of Evolving Family Commitment* (INSEAD case study, 2004).
2   Carlock, R. S. and Van der Heyden, L. "Board recognition and reward," *Families in Business*, January–February 2008.

3   Carlock, R. S. and Van der Heyden, L. "Natural selection: How to choose the best board," *Families in Business,* January–February 2008.

9 Family Governance: Family Meetings and Agreements

1   Carlock, R. S. and Florent-Treacy, E. *From Swords to Ploughshares: Three Generations of Family Entrepreneurship, Conflict, Transition and Connection* (INSEAD case study, 2009).
2   Kets de Vries, M. *Family Business: Human Dilemmas in the Family Firm* (London: International Thomson Business Press, 1996).
3   Speaking at the Kellogg School of Management Family Business Conference 2006.

10 The Men and Women Who Plant Trees

1   Giono, J. *The Man Who Planted Trees* (Condé Nast, 1954, originally published in *Vogue* under the title "The man who planted hope and reaped happiness"). The story was re-titled in 1982 and in 1987 became an animated film of the same title.

Index